Curling to Win

Ed Lukowich Al Hackner Rick Lang

With contributions from Ed Werenich and Marilyn Darte

McGraw-Hill Ryerson Limited

Toronto Montreal New York Auckland Bogotá Cairo Guatemala Hamburg Lisbon
London Madrid Mexico New Delhi Panama Paris San Juan São Paulo Singapore Tokyo

ISBN 0-07-549442-6

 5 6 7 8 9 10 W 5 4 3 2 1 0

Printed and bound in Canada

Canadian Cataloguing in Publication Data

Lukowich, Ed, 1946–

 Curling to win

ISBN 0-07-549442-6

1. Curling.   I. Hackner, Al.   II. Lang, Rick.
III. Title.

GV845.L84 1986   796.9'6   C86-094948-6

Photographs credited M. B. appear by courtesy of Mike
Burns Photography, Toronto.

Photographs credited A.W. appear by courtesy of Albert
Wong of A Hi-Tech Photography, Calgary.

The cartoons are by Frank McCourt.

Cover Art Direction by Daniel Kewley.

Cover illustration by Marc Mireault.

Contents

The Authors

Ed Lukowich "Fast Eddie" is co-author, along with Paul Gowsell and Rick Folk, of *The Curling Book,* published in 1981 and currently available in Canada, Scotland, Switzerland, Sweden and Japan. Ed is a former Canadian high school champion and has competed in four Briers, winning in 1978 and 1986. He won the 1986 World Curling Championship. Calgary is his home.

Al Hackner In four Brier appearances, "The Ice Man" has played every time in a sudden-death final. In 1982 and again in 1985 he won the Canadian Brier and the World Championship (Silver Broom). Al is well known for pressure shooting and "come from behind" victories. His teams represent the best in ability, sportsmanship and sociability. He lives in Thunder Bay, Ontario.

Rick Lang Rick has competed in six Briers and has won three. In addition he competed in three World Championships, winning two Silver Brooms as the third for Al Hackner. He also skipped a Canadian Mixed winner. His accomplishments reveal a wealth of experience at the highest curling levels. Rick was instrumental in setting up the famous "Heart to Heart Bonspiel" as a charity event in Thunder Bay, his home.

Foreword

BY HECTOR GERVAIS

Flashback: The Brier final, in 1985. Al Hackner, "The Ice Man," found a way to win—an incredible double kill to count two points for the tie and then steal the extra end. "The Hack came back," and who will ever forget Rick Lang using his brush and arms as body English, trying to coax the stone to curl that extra half-inch for the double.

That was perhaps the most memorable shot ever in a Brier. However, it was not the only comeback ever fashioned by Hackner. In 1982, after losing the Brier finals in 1980 and 1981, Al's team came back for a third consecutive try and went on to win the Brier and then the Silver Broom.

Flashback: "Fast Eddie" and his Canadian team in trouble at Toronto in the 1986 Silver Broom. With ice conditions favouring the hitting game, this draw team found a way to switch their game to the hitting style and win out over a tough David Smith from Scotland.

Like Hackner, Ed lost a Brier final in 1983, the semifinal in 1984 and the Alberta final in 1985. Finally in 1986 his team was able to come back and win the Brier final and overcome a Scottish team which had posted a 10-0 record going into the final of the World Championship.

Take it from the "Friendly Giant" from St Albert: in Ed, Al and Rick you have a wealth of curling knowledge that certainly places them in a position to help other players. They are well qualified to write this book.

Hector Gervais has skipped in four Briers and two World Championships.

M.B.

Al Hackner's 1982 championship rink in the Brier final against Gilles from B.C.

M.B.

Preface

Curling to Win, authored by "Fast Eddie," the "Ice Man" and his third, Rick Lang, is directed towards curlers who are already proficient at the game but wish to improve. It is aimed at the individual curler in the context of team play. We have purposely skipped the fundamentals of curling that are already common knowledge to the experienced curler. (The novice level of curling is covered in *The Curling Book,* by Ed Lukowich, Paul Gowsell and Rick Folk.) This book focusses on suggestions for improvement, problem-solving situations, higher-level strategy and little secrets of success.

While providing advice, the book presents curling in its most interesting form: it is a social game, with friendships at every turn and humorous situations the norm.

The main goal of the book is to help curlers improve their game so they can win more games by doing more things correctly. Just as golf experts have recognized that you can't force all people to swing one exact way, and that a certain person or body type may find a more comfortable and successful method, curling also makes room for individuality. The very best players have excellent style, but thrown in are some of the special techniques that they have discovered work well for them.

We hope that much of what you read here will help your game, but your own innovations may be just as good or better. It's the results that count.

ED, AL AND RICK

Section 1 *Introduction*

Winning

Where there is a will…

...there is a way!

In the pictures Wayne Hart is the thrower.
Stu Erickson (striped sweater) and Frank
Morrissette are the sweepers, while Dennis
Shupe directs traffic.

M.B.

"Carry them away."

M.B.

"Use the muscle."

"Take that."

"In case the roof falls in…"

All M.B.

"Better cheer louder!"

"Break their hand."

"Unconditional surrender!"

All M.B.

"Put your best foot forward."

"We shall wrench our way to the top."

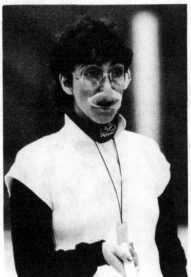

"Blow them away...

...till our bubble bursts."

"Pretend you really care."

M.B.

"Boots Labonte move over!"

M.B.

"Start with a glass of accuracy."

M.B.

"Use some body English."

All M.B.

"Try to distract them."

"Show a little leg."

"Knock 'em cold."

"Don't get excited."

"His wife wouldn't let him out of the house."

"Use invisible rocks."

"Practise self-hypnosis."

M.B.

"Try both barrels."

M.B.

The 1986 Brier, where 12 teams competed.

Teams

Curling has undergone many memorable changes. While technology has played its role, curlers, in their pursuit of excellence, have utilized new ideas in technique and strategy.

The greatest achievers in curling used uncanny insight to introduce a winning weapon: Ken Watson introduced the slide, and shooting drastically improved; the Richardsons, along with the hitting game, showed the biggest single winning factor, team unity; Matt Baldwin and Bud Somerville injected a flair for the dramatic; Ron Northcott brought back drawing and strong corn-broom sweeping by Sparkes and Storey; Hec Gervais forced the side guard game; Vera Pezer and Joyce McKee proved that the women could play well; Chuck Hay and Christian Soerum showed the

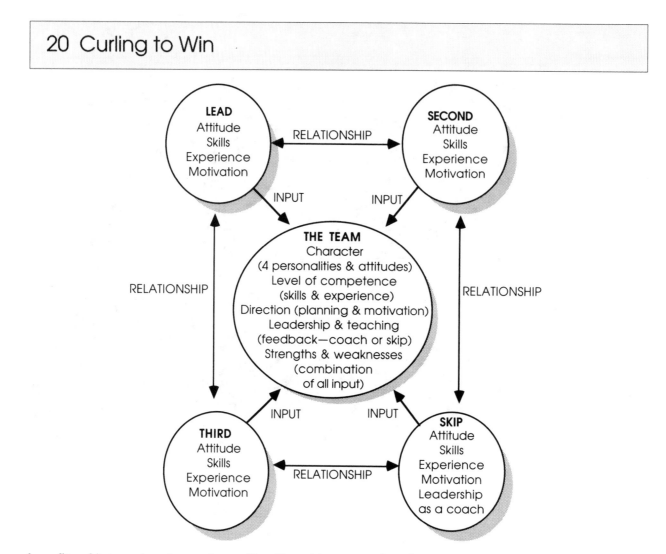

benefits of international experience; Don Duguid demonstrated what a strong balanced team could achieve; Paul Gowsell defeated the corn brooms and made the push broom ever popular; and Ed Werenich and Al Hackner have been recent winners because of the team unity factor (they combined their own shooting abilities and experience with their thirds', who are of equal stature and talent; and the latest trend, the high percentage shooting front end).

Who will be the next great innovator? One thing is for certain, the perimeters are expanding as curling grows.

To be successful and innovative in today's game, the strong team has to combine all the talents of their predecessors: drawing, hitting, sweeping, judgement and intangibles such as concentration, determination, confidence, nerve and experience. Ah yes, experience, the daddy of them all, for without it, even the silkiest shooting can roughen up. Ken Watson* said it best. "A team is only as strong as its weakest link," and that has never been truer than today.

When a large number of teams are combined they may appear to be quite similar. However, there are distinct differences in character and skill level among teams. The more you watch them in competition the more evident these differences in character will become, because the team is made up of individuals.

*Ken Watson is considered the father of Canadian curling and his book *Ken Watson on Curling* (1945) was a bible to Canadian curlers for many years.

M.B.

In 1986 the Muyers brothers, from Humboldt, Saskatchewan, were a Brier threat. The last all-brother team to win the Brier was the Campbells from Avonlea, Saskatchewan, in 1955.

On any team the team leader will be obvious. The leader influences the input of every player.

When we examine a particular team we find it to be composed of four players and possibly a coach. Any member of the team may have started it up; there is usually one person who took the initiative and asked the other players to join. This selection of the team is probably the most important decision that will be made. These players will be together on a regular basis to curl and what they achieve will depend upon all of the members.

Once all team members begin to have input you will notice that the foursome you are observing is taking a direction. The team will have a character that is formed by a combination of the personality and attitudes of all. Its character will determine the leadership roles and the other roles. You are fortunate if you have several members of the team who can supply leadership—sometimes direct, like that of a skip, or at other times indirect, in a quiet but productive manner.

The level of confidence the team acquires is determined by the skill and experience the players contribute to the unit. Each player will have a certain fitness level and a wide range of skills and abilities to add.

Such skills include throwing the rock accurately, judging and sweeping and a great variety of fine-tuned skills that are involved in the game. The experience factor will be made up of the members' life experiences, along with the number of years they have been curling and the level of competition that they have encountered.

The direction that the team will take is certainly dependent on the competence or lack thereof, as well as the motivations of the four people involved. Some teams might want to play just for the fun of it, while others might want to combine some pleasure with a little competition and see what they can accomplish. Others may go straight for the top. In that case, they become a very complex unit with every detail of the game becoming critical. Motivational input by each player grows vital. Remember, a team is only as strong as its weakest link.

When teams decide to improve, coaching becomes another factor. On most teams a skip plays the dual role of skip and coach, as he is usually the leader. His system of play will be used the most. The skip, with the help of his team members' input, will try to devise a plan of action that will work most effectively. This plan will be a combination of many different finer points in the game, such as strategy, improved throwing, calling the rock and all of the elements that determine the outcome of the game. It is essential for a team that the skip take control and be a leader and a teacher to develop the best plan of attack, so that the team is a unit and does not scramble along the way. He must be able to pick up quickly the weaknesses of the team and try to improve these, or use the players' strengths to achieve the most success.

From time to time throughout the season changes must be made for improvement, taking into consideration the rights and respecting the opinions of all the team members. Any time there is a breakdown in this trust and communication as a unit, the confidence and comradeship of the team will diminish and yield a less successful season. In other words, as a skip you must be a good coach and listener, letting all members have a slice of the action. Then, and only then, will you be successful.

There is nothing tougher in curling than dragging a body. It's like the story about golfing. Tom came off the course and was asked, "What kind of a game did you have, Tom?" "It was going very well," said Tom, "but on the fourth hole George had a heart attack." The other fellow replied, "Oh, that's terrible!" Tom said, "Yeah. Did you ever have to play fourteen holes, hit the ball, drag a body, hit the ball, drag a body?"

As the members of your team have input, they learn and continue to give more to the character and strength of that unit. If there is a point when that motivation fades and they have to be "dragged" to practice or to any of the games, then the unit as a whole is weakened. Thus the input of each member is a key in the relationships that form and gel as a team.

Input as an individual and response as a unit make the game that much more fun and rewarding. It goes without saying: "A team that plays together stays together." It is much easier to play and enjoy curling if you feel that you have responsibilities to the team and that you do belong.

While we have mostly discussed input to the team by the players, what does the team give to the players? It is the relationship one with another, the love of the game and the love of competition. There is the satisfaction of belonging to a team sport and a competitive team.

It is the individual with which this book is concerned. We look at one person, the member of the team, and suggest ways of improving his personal curling game, such as attitudes, skills, motivation, concentration, confidence and so on. By reading our tips, individuals, we hope, can speed the growth of their personal curling experience and also try out ideas that they may never have encountered. When you have four such individuals on a single team, all heightening the quality of their input, the team stands to gain strength and win more games.

Curling is a very social sport and this individual goal to improve has to be contained within the context of having fun. If you are too serious you force your teammates to withdraw and have less input. But if you are increasing your input and if you are fun to be around, then your teammates will want to contribute more as well. So improve, but have fun with the sport.

Section 2
Improving Your Game

"Slepp!!!"

The Skaugum Cup, Norway

Your Delivery

A smooth silky slide is a thing of beauty. Whether it is the flat-footed slide, heel-raised slide or the toe slide is totally a matter of personal preference and physical abilities. Top-notch players are not overly interested in the aesthetics of their slide but consider it simply a vehicle to complete the shot successfully. A championship player thinks of the finer points during a game and totally forgets the delivery.

When a player normally averages 80 to 95% in shooting success (we must consider experience, feel, icing, sweeping and calling as factors as well), it indicates a very solid delivery. The shooter has control of the stone and his body throughout the delivery.

An analysis of deliveries outlines varying slides, backswings, grips on the handle and releases. All of these are fine if they work for the individual; however, there are certain keys to look for in everyone's delivery, in order to see if the top-notch qualities are in place. Let's take the delivery through set-up, backswing, downswing, slide and release, and concentrate only on the keys (the factors that really matter).

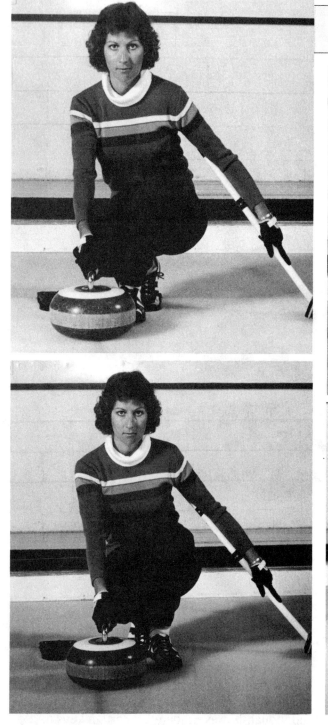

Hips—if the front foot moves over too much in front of the body, the hips will point too far to the right, as shown in the top photo. Reposition the foot to straighten the hips towards the broom, as in the bottom photo. Jill Ferguson demonstrates.

Shoulders—keep the shoulders as level as possible so that the centre of balance is directly over the foot in the hack. The posture shown in the top photo is fairly good, whereas in the bottom photo (John Ferguson) the centre of gravity is too close to the rock.

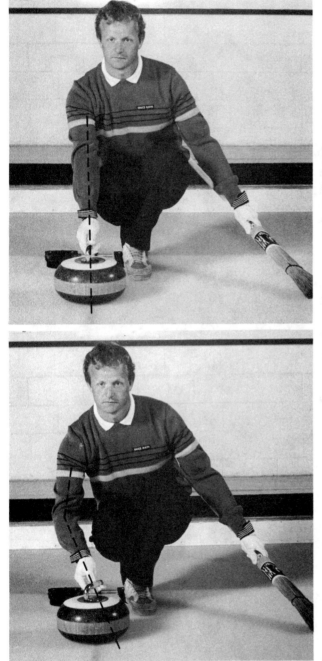

Rock—allow the hand to bisect the rock, as in the top photo. The bottom photo shows the arm not bisecting the rock and this leads to a flying elbow.

The top photo (1985 Canadian Junior Men's Champion Kevin Martin) is an excellent example of continuing to bisect the back of the rock, also during the slide. As the second photo shows, Paul Savage does not follow this rule. However, he has a release that works well for him and has a great feel for the shot *and six purple hearts*.

The backswing—bisect the rock. In the top photo, the stone is too far behind the leg. Note the better, straighter backswing in the bottom photo.

The downswing—bisect the rock. The top photo shows the stone too close inside the player's body. In the bottom photo, the stone is too far outside the player's body. (In both cases, the hand will not bisect the back of the rock.)

M.B.

Notice that Jim Armstrong's shoulders have remained rather level, allowing for a nice straight slide. Do not let the right shoulder drop too low on the downswing, or the delivery will go off balance.

Sliding foot—half of the rock. During the slide, as illustrated here, imagine the sliding foot behind your left half of the rock (left, that is, from the thrower's view, for a righthander).

A young U.S.A. champion, Scott Brown, in a toe slide. His style is different, as the sliding foot and trailing leg are off to the side. However, the right shoulder, the head and the eyes are definitely behind the stone. This type of delivery works well for some curlers.

In practice take each key factor of the delivery and develop it as a *good habit*.

A smooth slide is pure gold, and even more so if the results are stupendous. A top swing allows the stone to be thrown "at the broom" and during the heat of battle it can be relied upon to function automatically, so that the player can concentrate on the finer points of the game.

"At the Broom"

This may sound like kindergarten—"throw the rock at the broom." However, very few curlers can do it. Most players have the rock follow a slightly different pattern. Left and righthanders are direct opposites.

The diagram shows the normal pattern due to natural swing. Backswing is slightly away from the body, downswing is slightly into the body, correction is made at the release point and the rock is slightly crossed over the imaginary line. Inturns curl. Outturns run straight.

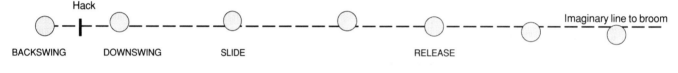

Hack

BACKSWING   DOWNSWING   SLIDE   RELEASE   Imaginary line to broom

(for a right-hander)

In the majority of cases, the backswing is slightly away from the body. On the critical downswing the rock dips in on the body and by the release point the thrower can either cross the target line causing an inturn to be turned (the rock will curl very early and continue to curl), or an outturn to straighten (the rock will fight the curl, and run quite straight). Thus, the stone is not thrown straight at the broom, but rather on a slight angle.

First and foremost, it is important to realize that this natural tendency exists. Learn to use it to your advantage in your delivery, in icing of teammates, and in using certain types of ice effectively.

The key is two-fold. Do *not* let this natural tendency, as illustrated in the next diagram, to become too exaggerated or else you are in for big delivery problems. Yet on the other hand, do not work so hard on totally correcting it that you get analysis paralysis, and start to do far too many corrections; if you begin flipping your releases, for example, then you will not throw at the broom at all and the stone's path down the ice will fight the natural curl. So let the backswing be natural, but correct it occasionally so it does not get extremely off line. A swing and delivery that are 90% on line will make many shots. Once you have achieved a much-improved delivery, you can concentrated on refining your game further.

How should a stone react? If the player has a straight swing and the rock can be released "at the broom" without any steering, the rock will react. If it is two or three inches wide, and not swept, it will react and curl. If the release is narrow, the sweeping will hold it straight. A rock thrown "at the broom" can be swept effectively.

You will know if you are throwing "at the broom" because your rock will react extremely well to the sweeping calls. It is an honest rock.

Because the backswing can be either out or in on the body, the stone can have many different problems with different players. The goal is a straight backswing. Take your delivery to the doctor for a monthly check-up by either using a player at the first hog who will sight the swing for you, or videotaping your performance. Cure the bad habits early. Your goal should be to reach a point where you can throw the rock "at the broom."

A backswing that is inside (behind the body) at its top can be detrimental because it leads to very erratic releases (variety here is not the spice of life) and poor shooting percentages. On the down-

M.B.

In this photo, Linda Moore, 1985 Ladies' World Champion, shows a number of practices at their best. The wrist bisects the back of the stone; the sliding foot overlaps half of the stone, and the slide has excellent height.

swing the rock tends to head out (wide from the body) and often the shoulders will follow, meaning an off-line slide. The rock usually starts wide on the downswing but is quickly jerked to the inside and from there the slide is off line and the release is not pretty. If your video shows some of the rock hiding behind (curving around) your leg on the backswing, it's time to begin work on it.

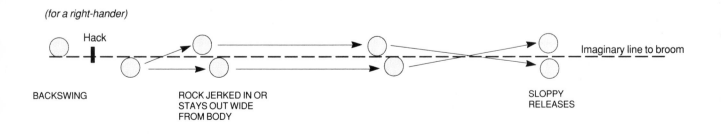

(for a right-hander)

Hack

Imaginary line to broom

BACKSWING

ROCK JERKED IN OR
STAYS OUT WIDE
FROM BODY

SLOPPY
RELEASES

Slides

1

M.B.

2

M.B.

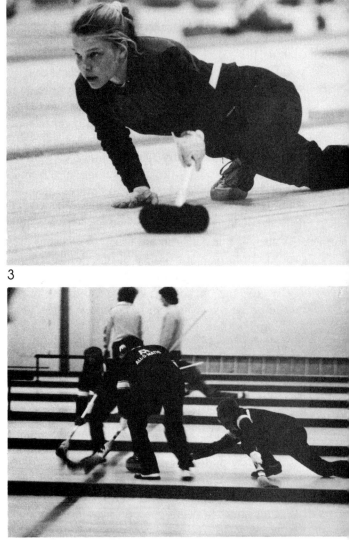

3

4

Type A—Flat-foot Slide

This type of slide is strongest for takeout. Photo 1 shows the slide with the brush bristles down to the ice. This is good for feeling the ice, but watch out when the ice is frosty, as there may be too much grab of the brush bristles against the ice.

Type B—Toe Slide

This type of delivery is equally effective for takeout or draw, depending upon the height of the slide. Higher slides are better for draw. An example is Rick Lang in photo 2. In photo 3 Andrea Schöpp of Germany rests the wood part of the brush against the ice.

Type C—The Raised-heel Slide

The best for draw weight, as the sliding foot is right under the body as shown in photo 4 (Rick Folk throwing, with sweepers Jim and Tom Wilson at 1980 World Championships), rather than reaching ahead as is normal with the flat-foot slide.

The raised-heel slide is the easiest on the sliding knee, while the toe slide applies the most pressure to the knee.

Timing

Timing is a very important part of the delivery. When the delivery is in the groove, there is excellent timing. Practise your timing by allowing both arms to go back simultaneously in the backswing, then let both arms and the sliding foot come forward together. Do this with or without a rock to improve your timing. The photo at the right shows the proof of good timing: the sliding foot, shoulders and arms are all in excellent position—John Kawaja, second on Ed Werenich's 1983 Men's World Champions.

M.B.

Secrets to Ed "the Wrench" Werenich's Delivery

In the sequence of photos that follows you will notice that as the delivery starts my head is in a relatively high position. I find that with this high position I have a very good perspective on the speed of my delivery and this helps me to get the rock in the "sweet spot." Since my arm is not stiff, I have an exceptional opportunity for the draw shots and soft shots that are required in the aggressive and competitive curling to which we are constantly exposed.

You can see in the photos that as the delivery progresses the arm extends, allowing me to get the required touch for the shot. If the rock is held too close to the body in the delivery there is a tendency to push the rock and lose your feel. If you hold the rock in front of your body with a stiff arm, it is almost impossible to adjust the feel and develop a constant weight for the shot. Next to a good delivery, one of the most important aspects of the game is feel. Really successful teams depend on the communication and execution of standard weights because of the variety of shots needed and differing ice conditions that teams face.

The other aspect of a solid delivery and probably the most difficult to master is a consistent release of the rock. If an inconsistent release is used it becomes very difficult to read the ice properly and therefore execute critical game-winning shots. As you can see, because I extend my arm as the delivery progresses, I have an accelerating release. This is very similar to a putting stroke in golf. Pro golf teachers stress the importance of accelerating through the ball so you have a good feel and release of the putter head (for our purposes, the handle of the rock). You can understand how important this technique is in curling, because you are required to throw turns, whereas in golf speed and direction are the primary concerns.

Dragging my right knee on the ice allows me to maintain good balance. It has another advantage too. The fast materials that we use on our shoes improve our hitting ability, but they can also mean that we come out of the hack too quickly on draw shots. Rather than slide over the hog line, in order to slow down and kill the accelerating effect, I just put a little pressure on my knee to slow myself down appropriately. The slightly raised heel is a result of the extension of the sweet spot at the end of my delivery, so I can keep it smooth and maintain maximum feel.

Practice

BY AL HACKNER AND RICK LANG

Practise, practise, practise. Over the years of curling and the games played, practice still shines through as a very useful means of improving the win-loss ratio. Good curlers are capable of walking out on the ice and making 70% of the shots. But many games are decided by *one* shot. Thus, if each player on a team can make one or two more shots per game, victory is so much easier.

Practice, along with plenty of games, can take care of the little things that can really make a difference. The axiom that "the game is half won in practice" is true. Teams that know how and what to practise can eliminate many mental errors and drastically improve their on-ice efficiency.

M.B.

The Stefan Hasselborg team (Sweden) warming up.

What are the immediate goals of practice? To make those one or two extra shots, to add more quality shots, to improve the systems of teamwork, to become machine-like in the fundamentals, to rehearse the game situations? All of these goals combined do one thing; they give you a distinct edge over the other teams you will play.

Team Practice

The types of practices that can be held are endless, and the members setting the practices should introduce variety into them.

Generally, one practice held every day or every other day is fine, although before a big event try to have one individual practice a day and one team practice. Two practice sessions a day are best.

If you practise, take the time to warm up properly. Do the stretching and the numerous practice slides and sweeping drills you use to warm up before a game. You will find this enhances the success of your practice and ensures a smooth entry into it.

During this warm-up, mentally go over the agenda and the good habits to be cultivated. Build the practice around the development of these good habits and this in turn will help to build your confidence. If you garner one, two or three good habits per practice, within a relatively short period of time you will be heading in the proper positive direction. Ask for constructive criticism when you have someone help you with your delivery, but build on the positive thereafter.

Often in a game a shot may be missed because you were out of position. For example, a front end player didn't stay with the rock all the way when sweeping; a third ran out to sweep when it was not necessary; a skip did not chase his draw and get right behind it to help the front end players. In practice, work on proper positioning for various shots and situations. It's these little things that can make a difference.

A total team practice is an excellent chance to work on systems. Such systems include the decision-making process, the strategy system, the methods of making suggestions, and the sweeping and calling systems. (Refer to the section on Systems, p.43.)

The skip or another member of a team can often pick out a slight problem the team is

"If this was bowling, that would have been a perfect gutter ball."

M.B.

Individual Practice

Cultivate the good habit of concentration. Pick out an imaginary broom and concentrate your attention on that spot. This is more difficult than normal and is excellent practice. Play one-on-one against yourself, and pretend you're in the big game. In every play, pretend you are in the final game and there is tremendous pressure. In many ways you are previewing the situations you can expect in the real games. Rehearse the pressure shots in this manner. Then throw all draws and see how many of the 16 rocks you can put in the rings. This grooves the delivery into remembering draw weight.

All hits: draw one in and throw hits. Try to hit and stay. If you roll out, then you have to play another draw. When you can throw a draw followed by 15 takeouts (all hit and stay), you can consider yourself a hitter. This also gives you a chance not only to read the ice, but to develop confidence in believing your own ice.

One-on-One

A four-end game against a teammate, designed for competitiveness and trick shooting. Rules: from near the hack, closest to the first button for the hammer and no peeling of front stones when ahead in the score.

After many years of playing each other in one-on-one, it became more difficult for us to make appropriate bets. The ultimate solution was to play for "all the money in the world." This imaginative prestige item was symbolized by a sack of chocolate gold coins which remained in the possession of the current champion. Despite no actual value being involved, this method served to keep interest high as we always had a reigning singles champion.

having during a game and offer a good solution. Keep notes on the suggestions you come up with and use them in your next schedule game. Thus, the schedule games themselves can work as a positive session aimed at a particular improvement.

Start the practice with five minutes of calisthenic warm-ups, and add slides and a few throws back and forth to get the feel. Now you are ready to begin. Decide on a very definite type of practice and the goal(s).

The key to practice is to develop good habits. Every practice, decide on the good habit(s) to cultivate. All teams are rather rough at the beginning of the year. But the teams that can grow and develop good habits are the ones that are around at the end.

Two-on-Two

A four-end game in which the team plays two against two. Rules: no peeling when ahead and sweeping allowed, but partner must hold broom first. This lets you see how players are throwing. Fancy shots are practised by everyone.

In Scotland, two-on-two is a standardized game with regular leagues of men, women and mixed. There are also national pairs champions declared for the country. Imagine you and your teammate as pairs champions.

Corners

A variation of two-on-two. Play three days in a row. Each day take a different player for your partner. Every day the winning team gets 10 points. The one player with the most points after three days is the champion.

M.B.

"One is too many, and 100 is not enough!"—Ron Thompson, Vancouver.

No-Rocks Practice

Have a player hold the broom just past the first hog line. Practise sliding at the broom (from one extreme side to the other). This gets the body coming out at the broom correctly. Do this once in a while to revitalize your slide. Do a whole session of sliding without the rock to straighten your slide. Practise intentionally sliding a little wide and then a little narrow. This little experiment may help you discover that your attempt to slide straight at the broom is actually a narrow or wide one.

Delivery Checks

To check your delivery, use a video or ask a player to hold the broom just beyond the first hog line. The most important point to observe is the downswing. Is the rock on line as it touches down on the ice, and in the first five feet of the slide? Most curling shots are missed in this area of the slide. If your downswing is off line, refer to the section on delivery.

Ports

Set up rocks at the hog line with a port of 14 inches. Use each turn until three consecutive rocks pass cleanly through. Place the rocks further away to increase the degree of difficulty. This is excellent practice for your release.

In preparation for certain ice conditions, it is better to practise on similar ice. Your judgement on sweep and your feel for throwing will be much better from this familiar practice. Club playdowns are often the most difficult, because club curlers are very good on their own ice after playing on it all year.

Pregame Practice

Nowadays, in several bonspiels, in provincial playdowns and in playdowns of national and world levels, teams are allowed to practise before the game on the sheet that they will play on. This is beneficial because teams are able to catch the ice quicker and play much better in the first and second ends, when the pebble has already been broken down and they have already found a good feel for draw weight. So take advantage and get out there and use your practice time.

Our own team tries to practise as many shots as we can in the 10 or 15 minutes that are allotted to us. We try to time draw shots close to the end of our practice when the pebble is finally broken down. We also like to pre-test the rocks that we will use in the game (see p.93) and that also helps.

Taking advantage of the pregame practice also means that your team will be either the first or second team to practise on that sheet. If you get to practise first, be sure that you time some of the rocks that your opposition throws on the ice after you practise. By the end of their 10- to 15-minute practice, the ice may have keened up 10 feet or more than when you practised, since the pebble is increasingly worn down. For example, you are playing the first draws of the game, and your lead isn't pitching them into the hack but rather he has good timing and a good feel for draw weight.

In most cases, after the final practice on that sheet the ice is not re-pebbled. Most times it is recleaned and then the players come out and play on that ice just as it was at the completion of the final practice. So the weight, or the timing of draw shots, will be pretty well exactly as it was during the final practice. Other than that, the only time the ice is cleaned is usually during the fifth–end break.

That fifth-end break was originally inserted in the rules so that people who wanted to run out for a smoke could do so. But that isn't really the reason why it is done nowadays. Certainly the

"Do you think that we will ever get it right?"

ice is cleaned halfway through the game, but the break is actually an excellent opportunity for the team to get off the ice and discuss exactly how their game is going. It's also the perfect time for a coach to talk to his players, to reassess and to plan the last five ends of the game.

Practice Summary

The following is a list of fundamentals to work on in practice. These are points that are particularly difficult to do much about during a game:

The delivery—In most cases you are your own doctor, and the prescription is always to work on alignment for accuracy and then throw plenty of rocks for the feel of the ice. In practice, build good habits in your delivery. We are creatures of habit and they are either good or bad. It's the good habits that you wish to incorporate as machine-like in your style.

The doctor—Periodically ask your teammate to examine your slide up close and directly in front. If there is a problem, it will appear in your downswing or in your ability to slide accurately at the broom.

Everyone seems to have the ability to slide well at the broom without a rock in their hands; however, add the rock and a crooked swing, and the slide can be far off line. Read the section on the swing (p.26)—it's the key to accuracy.

Forgetting the delivery—At the end of practice, before the game, practise forgetting the delivery. As in golf, during the game you cannot become preoccupied with the swing. There are too many other things going on, too much else to observe and calculate; it's then that you want your delivery to be automatic so that you can concentrate on the game itself. (Read the section on delivery, p.23.)

The team meeting practice—every month or so, have a team meeting on the ice where you get away from practising shots, and review team fundamentals.

1. Review the systems you are using in games and be sure everyone knows their job and how to communicate with one another.

2. Review your general strategy and the positioning of various shots, along with the signals that are used for every shot, weight and positioning, from the skip to the shooter.

With all the team play, work on establishing effective communication. Try to eliminate the minor errors.

A Conditioning Program

BY TEAM LUKOWICH

"Yes," replied the third, "we trained. The front end and I pumped iron. The skipper pushed aluminum."

What we look for in the curler is lean, strong, flexible endurance muscles that hold top quality muscle tone. Almost all other sports, with their physical and mental practice, can be of direct aid to your curling training. In this respect, curling offers a major advantage.

Front end players need strength for hard sweeping, coupled with high levels of endurance to sweep the length of the ice for possibly three games per day.

The third is a combination player, at times requiring the strength and endurance of a front end player, while being able to be a great finesse player.

The skip is in a finesse position, primarily, and he requires a high level of muscle tone, but not bulk muscle.

Because today's team demands four good finesse players, the front end players also need exercises that concentrate on stamina and high level muscle tone.

One fitness program can be used by all four players on the team. The program should be based upon endurance training, possibly including more weight training for the front end players.

The following sports will help your curling:

Golf—closely related to curling in the mental aspects, the swings (delivery), the accuracy and feel of the shots and putting (reading the ice). This sport builds up leg muscles and stamina. Golf is a highly mental and physical test, much like curling.

Jogging, cross-country skiing and biking—all these sports build body tone, leg endurance for sweeping, leg strength for delivery, cardiovascular strength for sweeping. Recommended for all four players.

Squash, racquetball, badminton, tennis—same benefits as jogging. In addition they build mental toughness, competitive drive. Recommended for all four players.

Swimming—excellent for total body tone. Recommended for all four players and especially the skip.

Hockey, skiing, diving and soccer—great for legs (kingpins of curling), highly recommended for building nerve, especially for skips; not recommended for accident-prone people.

Cards, chess, billiards—these intellectual games teach strategy and build mental sharpness.

CURLING ... A GAME OF BALANCE, GRACE, ... AND A BACKGROUND IN "BALLET" COULD "HELP".

How to Train

The exercises recommended below can be individualized easily, and require minimum equipment. Vary the number of repetitions, the number of sets, and the weights involved to match up with your own particular fitness level.

In a general circuit progression program, you increase repetitions in a daily "three set" program (repeating each exercise three times) to a maximum number of repetitions over several consecutive days. Then you increase the difficulty or weight, start low with your repetitions and gradually increase them again.

When setting up your personal program, chart your goals ahead of time. The goals you should aim for are these:

1) leg strength and endurance (for throwing and sweeping),

2) abdominal strength and tone (key muscle tone area for consistent delivery),

3) arm strength and endurance for sweeping,

4) upper and lower back muscle tone required for standing and moving about for three games per day.

This program is recommended equally for both sexes, and in fact especially for women. Because men are normally stronger than women, weight training through the progression program described here is the finest method available for women curlers to close up the strength gap between male and female curlers. Women are already known to be equal to men in endurance.

As you follow this program, alternate the arm and leg and abdominal exercises throughout the circuit. To begin the program you need access to a health club's training room, or an at-home set of the same type of equipment.

Recommendation: Please consult your physician before starting this program. Also, consult the weight room instructor if you are using a club's facilities. And don't do the heavy weight third set until you have been in the program for at least two weeks, or 10 sessions.

Warm-up

1) Spot running—good warm-up and endurance. Two minutes, build up to 10 minutes.

2) Stretching—use stretches similar to the pregame ones. Pregame stretches should be 10-15 minutes.

Circuit Exercises

1) Biking—Indoor bike. Use tension set and increase riding time. Excellent for additional

Racquet sports—
John Ferguson

Spot running—
Brent Syme

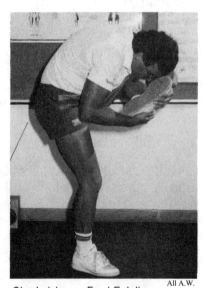

All A.W.

Stretching—Fast Eddie

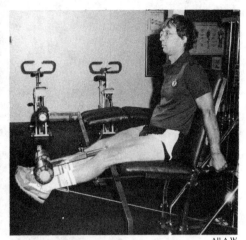

Cycling—Judy Lukowich   Sit-ups—Neil Houston   Front leg raises   All A.W

warm-up plus leg strength and endurance. Start with two minutes and build up to five minutes, then increase tension to next level.

2) Sit-ups—Start with five repetitions and build to 60. Increase difficulty gradually: hands under knees, hands on forehead, hands behind head.

3) Front leg raises—These build quadriceps. Start with six repetitions, progress to 12, then increase weight and start at six repetitions again.

4) Curls—For biceps strength. Start with 10 repetitions, increase to 20, then increase the weights and start again. Use the same program for the following three exercises.

5) Back leg raises—To tone hamstrings.

Curls

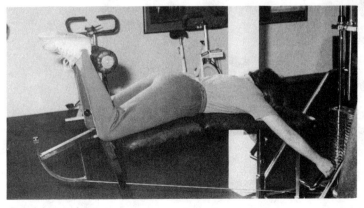

Back leg raises

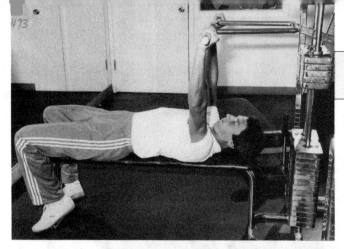

Bench press

Back raises

All A.W.

6) Bench press—Will strengthen arms and chest muscles.

7) Back raises—This is a reverse body curl for little-used back muscles.

8) Skipping—A tremendous conditioner for calf muscles. Start with 50 repetitions and climb to 300.

9) Pulldowns—Good for arms and shoulders, important for sweeping. Start with 10 repetitions, increase to 20, then increase weights and start back at 10 repetitions.

10) Sit-ups—Do these while leaning three-quarters of the way down. Tones the mid-abdominal muscles plus the side abdominals.

11) Easy biking and spot jogging slowly to cool down. Five minutes is a sufficient cool-down period.

Do the set three times, twice without heavy weights while building progressions. For the third round, use a heavy weight and only one or two repetitions.

A lead or second could do five to seven sessions per week. For a third and skip, keep it to three sessions. If you are afraid of bulk, do more abdominal exercises, skipping, squash, swimming, etc.

You can add many more circuit exercises to your program as you progress. Either use your own initiative or consult your local fitness director.

Skipping

Pulldowns

Sit-ups

M.B.

Hritzuk vs Hackner, 1985 Brier.

Systems

Systems in curling enhance the level of team play and help to organize everyone's thinking.

Making Decisions

For shot selection, elect your most experienced player to use the "first reaction method."

As soon as the other team's rock has stopped, a brand-new situation arises; the person elected looks at the shot and flashes "a first reaction." Assuming this person is the third or the skip, immediately discuss this first reaction and decide if it truly is the best shot. Often if a first reaction isn't used, you'll stumble over deciding between two or three shots and end up selecting the

wrong one. There has to be a good strong reason for not playing the first reaction shot.

Because *all* the players on the team should have some say in shots selected, pick a spot about 15 feet outside the hog line for team meetings. If one players travels to that spot and studies the play, that is a signal for a team discussion. This discussion should be settled finally by a vote or by the intuition of the person who has to play the shot.

Always make your decision the same way: shot, then turn, then weight, then ice. That way a skip and a third follow the same sequence.

M.B.

Al Hackner and Rick Lang have had success with on-ice decisions. They think on the same wavelength. Each respects the other's opinion as much as his own.

Weight System

At the beginning of the season it is practical to set up a weight system with your team. It provides an excellent means of weight communication between players, so that each player knows about weight selection for every shot.

Use your home club as your basis to establish a standard weight system. The entire system should work with normal draw weight as the central axis. A suggested system appears below. (The numbers shown here indicate the hardness of the throw; the more weight required, the higher the number.)

1. Extremely keen ice.
2. Guard weight, keen spot.
3. Normal draw weight.
4. Back ring weight—five feet over normal.
5. Hack weight—10 feet over normal.
6. Bumper (board weight)—enough to reach the glass behind the sheet—15-18 feet more than draw.

7. Takeout (bumper plus 10 feet).
8. Peel weight (same as heavy takeout or more if thrown very free).
9. High hard one (peel weight plus, released at semi-early point in the rings).
10. Extra high hard one (peel weight double-plus released at early point in the rings).

When players communicate with one another by using such a method, it can help to settle confusion on weights. For example, in removing a guard, state whether it is to be #7 takeout or #8 peel.

It is particularly helpful when the high hard shot is needed. How hard are you going to throw? Try to be specific and not just fire it. It's also good on new ice. Your advice to a teammate might be, "it's keener," but what does that mean? It's better to say, "normal draw weight today is like two rather than three."

Although these numbers ask for a special weight—example, bumper—it is advisable to keep "feel" as a central part of the throw.

Other Systems

The weight system described above is only one of the systems used in curling. You still need to have a "feel" for draw weight, which is another system, and there are also many teams using the stopwatch system as well. (See the section on the stopwatch, p.100) The stopwatch is a system of timing. It works in an opposite way to the weight system just explained: the keener the ice, the greater the number time for a draw to travel the length of the ice. Many teams use all three ways—the weight system, the stopwatch and feeling the weight.

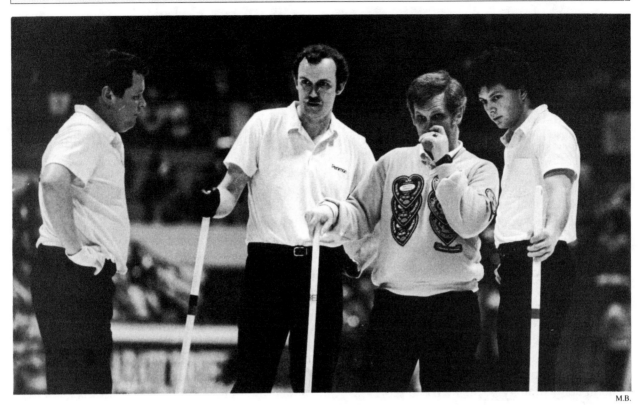

M.B.

The Ed Werenich team, 1983 World Champions: Left to right, Paul Savage, Neil Harrison, the Wrench, John Kawaja.

Strategy

The strategy of curling has changed over the years. In 1959, with Ernie Richardson of Canada throwing many takeouts, and Willie Young of Scotland playing nothing but the draw game, the Scots bitterly complained about the Canadian takeout game: "Nay, that ain't curling," they said.

In 1986 Scotland's David Smith was part of the strongest hitting team in the World Curling Championship with a 10-1 win-loss record. This was a total reversal of strategy from the Scots' 1959 game. In the interval, reviewing the years of Ron Northcott, Chuck Hay, Hec Gervais and Don Duguid, it is apparent that the draw game was used to defeat other teams.

Today, the toughest teams are precise hitters who combine that skill with tremendous strength at the draw game. It seems that some teams can master the hit game and add the finesse of a good draw game. The same strong draw teams don't give anything away at the takeout game either, and they end up at the top of the heap.

Thus, this section on strategy focusses on the draw game and how to use its strengths properly.

Before we go further, let's examine simple strategy. For years beginning curlers have been told to keep the front open when they have last rock, and especially peel the centre guards to keep the four-foot open. This is still true at times today, but you may see inexperienced skips who don't know when enough is enough. They can be two down in the game and need points badly, and yet they will be out there peeling off guards because someone told them to keep the front open for their last shot. Instead they should be drawing behind and going for a big end.

On the other hand, you will see skips, three up in a game, place their lead's first stone out in front of the rings because that is accepted practice. An opposition skip will say "thank you" and draw behind. He won't peel the guard, if he is experienced. The skip who is three up has shown that he does not know how to take the game into the rings.

Too many inexperienced skips do not know how to skip more than two types of ends, and that simply is not enough to get by on. Many don't know how to change their strategy during the match.

Learn to play a healthy game, hitting and drawing. Have a game plan in which four ends are takeout, three ends are draw and three ends are surprise ends (where you begin a certain strategy and change quickly midway through to trap the opposition).

A good question to ask yourself about your general team strategy is: do we try to score the points that win the game by stealing when they have the last rock, or do we go for good-sized ends when we have last rock? Certainly your answer will depend on your strength, the opposition, the score and the ice conditions. However, the game plan dictates that you win the game by scoring two with last rock and hold the opposition to a single when they have last stone. Win the game by scoring crucial points with the hammer.

Curling is a game of offence, defence, offence, defence. So to be able to score points with last rock you need to draw (you only peel off all the front rocks to keep it open half of the time, the other half you go on offence and draw). To play defence when the opponent has last rock, you often elect not to play a centre guard, but instead to place a stone in the rings and play a bumper weight hitting game.

The experienced skip is capable of using the old strategies, but he also has a whole new way of thinking about offence and defence.

Let's examine the various types of ends you are required to be able to skip in today's game, as the score dictates. The following is a play-by-play account of a game of curling using up 11 ends (this battle went an extra end). Thus there are 22 ends (11 by each skip) of strategy that can be shown. This game illustrates nearly all the situations that you will meet as you learn to skip.

We will play the dark rocks against the white rocks. The Darks won the toss but all things being equal, that last rock advantage is only issued for the Darks on the first end. Ten ends will follow to change all that.

White Rosey is asked by her skip White Honcho to place the first stone in front of the rings, about halfway between the hog and the front of the rings. The teams are playing on fresh pebble and she only passes over the hog line by one foot (almost had to buy a round). Sweeping didn't help much on the fresh pebble. (You have to throw it where you want it on fresh pebble).

Dark Angus was going to peel the guard if it came close to the rings and wait for his team to get the feel of the ice. However, this long guard offers a good draw-around opportunity to get a big end and a jump in the score. Dark Angus has decided not to keep the front open but rather gamble. Dark Julie draws behind to the button, half-visible (open).

The Whites play bumper weight, chip it out and roll out. Angus asks for a bury shot to the top ring and gets it.

Illustration 1 shows the negative effect of the Whites' long guard. The Whites play to remove the dark stone but because of its height in the rings it has to be wicked and must be passed through almost 12 feet of the rings, as compared to the former stone on the button which only had to be passed six feet out of the rings.

The removal of the stone at the top ring becomes more difficult in this situation and drawing to it is not ideal either. The Whites attempt to remove it but only manage to push it over to the side.

This is now an ideal situation for the Darks, as

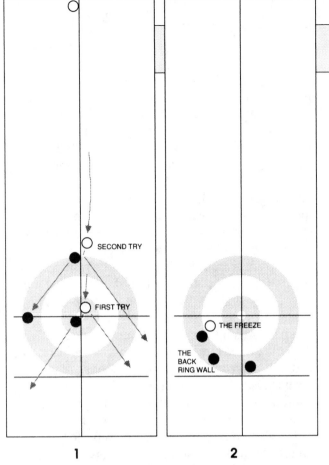

1   2

they have a side counter and draw again behind the guard. They are making quality shots. The Whites now try to draw to the dark counter, but the player is three feet heavy, thereby rubbing the stone and sliding into the open.

The Darks hit and maintain this advantage by making the remainder of their shots. The Whites fail to make a double to escape. The count is Darks 3.

End 1: The Whites try to go for the steal. Long guard backfires and the Darks gamble and make quality shots.

Here is how the Whites are thinking as they go into end two. Do we gamble right away to get back into it or do we show some patience? There are still nine ends left and Skip White remembers: When behind in a game, try to be, at the worst, two down playing the tenth end, so that you can get a two-ender and then steal the extra end.

The Darks, being three points ahead, decide to play it open and defensively for a while. They

place their first stone just touching the top of the four-foot on the centre.

The Whites are undecided. Do they play a side guard, or perhaps a freeze to get some points back? White Harry, the second, suggests that it's too early to panic. Play the takeout.

A few takeouts are exchanged and finally the Whites get a small break, as the Darks roll out. The Whites play a guard well off to the side in order to leave their skip plenty of room to draw with the last stone. The second is the toughest end in a game to draw. Ice can keen up so quickly and trails are very different at this point.

With the side guard, the Darks can peel it, place a centre guard or put a stone in the rings. Team preference dictates the choice here, as the Darks ask for a centre guard but slip into the rings with the second's last stone.

It turns out to be the worst shot as it was too early to draw into the rings with a side guard present. The Whites take out and roll behind the side guard—their first quality shot in the game.

Our White skip draws into the rings for two, as the Darks had missed one and been trapped by the side guard game. For his final shot, the draw for two, the skip takes the same path that the Darks' lead had played on the first shot of the end (draw to the top of the four) so he timed their shot on his stopwatch and took off a tiny bit for extra keenness. Usually skips don't take the weight for their shots off the lead's rocks in the early ends, as the ice can keen quickly during the end.

Score after two ends—Whites 2, Darks 3.

End 2: Saw patient side guard game from the Whites, and an unsuccessful attempt by the Darks to play a defensive, "in the rings" game.

The Darks are almost a good team. They made quality shots on the first end as they drew well on fresh pebble. They played to the top of the four-foot on the second end to control the game.

You see, as a team you want to indicate the strategy of the game. You want to draw only when you deem it advantageous. You want the game played in your own backyard.

A small error in the second end has let the Whites come back into the game. However, the Darks are still "one up with," the ideal strategy situation. They now can gamble, whereas the Whites can steal only one or give up a possible two or three end again. It has become easier now to set the trap.

End 3: Patient but boring.

The Whites' skip now looks at his pregame plan. Play four ends takeout, three ends draw, three ends of surprise tactics. He has yet to play a takeout end and has decided to put some health and freshness into this game by playing end three as a hit end. He asks his lead to follow the same trail as he himself did with his last rock on the second end. Thus the lead has just seen the weight in this path and successfully draws to the top of the eight-foot.

The Darks' skip would like to play some offence this end to reinstate the three-point lead, but he isn't that anxious to play a side guard or freeze just yet. So the team member replaces the Whites' stone and stays with takeout weight.

The Whites' skip has decided to use patience and not get three down again, there are still seven ends to go after this one. He decides, as the ice is now keening up, to have his team hit and stay with bumper weight, not roll out to give the Darks a chance for a side guard. His team finally plays a quality flawless end, hitting and staying, and drawing back in when the Darks rolled out with takeout weight.

Finally, in an unsuccessful attempt to blank, the Darks hit and stayed for one point.

Score after three ends: Darks 4, Whites 2.

The Darks certainly didn't lose the end. However, the failure to blank gives the hammer back to the Whites. The Whites consider the end a victory and now can go on the offence with the hammer in end four.

End 4: The Great Wall of China.

The Darks decide to play to the top of the eight-foot on the centre line and control the end with a takeout game in the rings. The Whites' skip knows their intention very well—after all, he just played that type of end himself.

There are a few choices open to him. He could take the stone out (not a bad strategy), and wait for the opponents to roll out and go with the side guard game. After all it did work in the second end. He could play a side guard right now (maybe the Darks would ignore it and try to guard their stone or draw around the side guard, Riley style), or perhaps a freeze would be in order.

But no. He elects to tap the opponents' stone to the back ring, as he feels his team now has good draw sense. His lead taps the Darks' stone to the back and sits for shot stone seven feet in front of it.

The Darks hit and stay while rolling slightly to the left. The Whites again tap this to the back ring and now have two of the Darks' stones at the back rings behind their counter. The Darks continue to hit well as the Whites play the tap-to-back ring game for their first four shots.

Illustration 2 shows what the house looks like on their third's first shot. The Darks have three stones at the back without last stone. Against a good skip these stones normally wouldn't count. Thus the Whites have built a good wall and a possible pocket to freeze into.

Freezes are undoubtedly among curling's finest shots, along with raises. See the section on freezes on p.84 to learn more about the team play involved in these shots.

The Whites position a "freeze" which is very difficult to remove. The Darks are now faced with one of curling's tough decisions. Considering the degree of difficulty, do they try to run the stone out past their own, or do they revert to the freeze game and now play right along with the Whites? It can backfire either way. And either way Whites now have the Darks conditioned to make decisions and finesse shots—"got them thinking."

The Darks try to run it out with big weight, unsuccessfully, and the Whites take two to tie the game. The Whites have now played three good ends in a row. As a bonus, the Whites' skip has successfully played the last shot of end two and four to put the points on the board that were available, making use of the opportunity as it knocked.

End 5: Kitty by the Door.

Finally the game is back where it began—tied and the Darks have the hammer. The Whites decide to exert a little pressure and play centre guards close to the rings. The Darks play safe and hit and roll for a side guard as they would like a side guard game with their last stone advantage (either get a deuce on the side or draw the "four" to save the end). The Whites don't want the side guard game and they peel the side guard. The Darks replace the side guard.

The Whites now remove the side guard and roll to the centre. The Darks play to remove the centre guard and fan it.

Now the draw game is on. Both teams play well around the centre, but the Darks have the hammer and they draw to the other stones at the back of the four-foot for one.

Score: Darks 5, White 4. Both teams have shown that they can now draw around centre guards. However, the Whites' skip has noticed a flaw in the Dark skip's delivery and he hopes to capitalize.

End 6: "Your Slip Is Showing."

The Darks want to play into the rings and force the Whites to a single point. Their attempt is close as they hit the top ring. The Whites' skip feels that a deuce with the hammer is now necessary to win this game and he gambles: he ignores the stone at the top ring and plays a side guard. The Darks successfully peel it.

The Whites' skip now uses the strategy least used by teams; he asks for a freeze to the shot at the top ring, and he stops about five inches short of it, outside of the rings.

The Darks have several choices. They can draw to the other side, draw to the button, play a centre guard or play the hit.

They play the hit and it does not work out well. The Whites' rock is driven on their own and rolled for a short side guard, while their shooter rolls to the other side. The Whites' skip

now places a guard slightly over the centre line to force the draw game to that side.

With three guards in play, the Darks decide to "go in first" with their draw. Several draws follow one another and finally the Darks' skip misses a key tapout.

It was a well-laid trap. The Whites' skip had noticed that flaw in the Dark skip's downswing. It was too much inside the body, forcing him to straighten his outturn release. That is why the Whites' skip positioned his early guard slightly off centre on the one side, to force the outturn draw game.

The result—a miss by the Darks' skip and a deuce for the Whites.

Score after six ends: Whites 6, Darks 5.

End 7: Panic time.

Darks had a three-love lead, but now they trail by one point after six ends. The Whites feel better now, but the game is far from over. The Whites' philosophy is to try to win most games by two or three points by gambling early in the game. But that backfired, as they played poorly in the first end and were down three points. Their philosophy is now to play control curling and win the game by 40 pounds (one stone, their last shot).

The Whites place the first stone in the top of the four-foot. (Their lead, White Rosey, has done a great job of positioning stones to start an end properly. This is a key to controlling strategy. Her only error was the overly long guard on the first end.)

The Darks break out two new straw brooms to litter the ice with straw bits. As they sweep with the two brooms their stone can't move through the fresh hay and it is hogged, as a side guard attempt, by 20 feet. The Whites play a very tight guard on their own stone, to control the top of the house (keeping the moving stone clean every inch of the way to avoid the straw).

The Darks' skip instructs his team to use one brush right next to the stone and a new corn broom out front. "Litter straw on the ice, but keep it away from our rock." The end continues, with the Darks trying to recover. The Whites do not take any extra time to clean the ice, but rather do a fine job of sweeping and keeping the stone clean. They play a good end by applying the pressure and have two buried in the four-foot by their finish of play. The Darks' skip makes a fine draw to the button to salvage the end.

Result: a tie.

The Whites wanted to play it simple, but once given the opportunity they changed to a tight guard game and forced the Darks to a tough single. The Darks panicked in strategy and made the mistake of bringing out the corn. However, the skip did make a great shot to salvage.

End 8: This End Should Win It.

Both teams realize the importance of scoring on the eighth end. It is the even end and scoring here might provide the hammer for the tenth end as well.

The Darks play five centre guards and the Whites peel them all. These teams are really shooting well. The Darks place a sixth centre guard. Perhaps they should have known that the Whites could not be trusted and that they should have placed their stone in the rings.

After a short discussion the Whites decide to draw behind. They have three rocks left to the Darks' two and they can "go in first." It is a change of strategy during the end, a well-known system, and if the surprise works it could give them a two-point lead. Their draw shot is too deep (back of the four-foot) and it affords the Darks' skip a come-around freeze.

He makes the freeze, the Whites make a freeze, the Darks make a freeze and are frozen on the button; the Whites cannot move it and the Darks steal one.

The Whites made a sweeping error of the third's come around, as once it was going behind the tee they should have swept it deeper yet, to the back eight-foot to avoid that build-up to the button freeze: lack of forethought.

Score: Darks 7, Whites 6. It is definitely not a totally defensive battle, but a very good game, with many fine shots made.

End 9: Strategy Pays Off.

The Darks play a smart strategy. Their first stone is a centre guard to force a decision. The Whites elect to peel. After a couple of peels the Whites finally roll for a side guard. The Darks ignore it and replay the centre guard. They don't want the blank end so they are forcing the issue. Finally the Whites decide to go in on the outturn around the centre guard and force the Darks' skip to play that outturn that he botched in the sixth end.

It works, and the Darks' skip rubs the guard and his shooter squirms into the rings for shot stone. The Whites' skip makes his first *faux pas* of the match as he rolls out for the deuce on nine—too much pressure, played too carefully. He doesn't get the deuce, doesn't get the blank. One point has been scored to tie the match, without the hammer going home.

End 10: So It's Come To This.

The Whites lay seven guards out front. The Darks peel them all off, as they throw big weight and are good peelers. Skip White plays his final stone behind the tee slightly to the side in the rings.

The Darks should draw the eight-foot to win the game (a draw to the eight-foot or the four-foot should be a routine shot for a skip by the tenth end, as an excellent feel for this weight should be developed), but the team chickens out and rolls out on the hit.

The third says, "Play the takeout. Even if you roll out we still have the hammer in the extra end." But he now realizes that ice conditions were good for the draw and the hit was in a tricky spot; this is probably why the Whites placed it there.

End 11: Extra End—The Great Pass Shot.

The Whites ask for a tight guard. The Darks hit it on the nose. The Whites ask for a long guard. They keep the separation between the stones to avoid the heavy weight double and roll off with the shooter. The Darks play to chip off either guard and peel off the short one.

The Whites now ask for a rock in the four-foot—"not behind the tee"—and give plenty of ice to be sure not to chip the guard. The skip will tighten the ice as he learns the spot. The Whites' third suggests playing another guard, but they decide to keep plenty of length between the long guard and the proposed shooter (avoid a double).

The White player half-buries the stone behind the long guard. The Darks run the front guard but hit it just off the nose and narrowly miss the double. Nothing has changed but the colour of the long guard. The Whites come right in again on top of their own.

The Darks now decide to follow and move back the stones in the four-foot. By the time the thirds come to shoot, it's trouble for the Darks. They try a triple but only get the short biter in the top of the house.

With their final stone, the Whites can either guard the raise or guard the draw to the button. Their experience leads them to decide to do neither.

The Whites throw their last stone away, leaving the Darks with a choice. The Whites have decided not to make up the mind of the Darks' skip but rather leave him a decision. That way even in the hack he may not be sure if the chosen shot is the best possibility.

Thus the Darks are left with a five-minute discussion. The lead and the second like the draw, the skip likes the raise, and the third hates himself for not letting the skip draw the eight-foot in the tenth end. Finally they elect the button draw and are just heavy for the loss.

The superior experience and patience of one team barely edged out the average experience and strong shooting of the other. Luck played only a small part, as the teams curled well and there weren't any major flukes.

In 11 ends of curling, the Whites' skip showed us plenty of variety. He skipped the following types of ends:

End 1—A steal end (didn't work because of poor execution).
End 2—Patient side guard game—waited for a chance to play the side guard.
End 3—Bumper-weight-in-the-rings-control-end; force opponent to a single.
End 4—Back ring wall set-up; freeze end—set up your deuce.
End 5—Tight guard game—played a tough end, kept pressure on.
End 6—Top house freeze game—set up the draw end.
End 7—Control top of house—looks for errors in opposition skipping.
End 8—Peel end; switch to draw late in end—a surprise end; "draw to your advantage."
End 9—Two-fold end; blank or get two.
End 10—A steal end—forced blank from opposition.
End 11—An excellent steal end—avoided doubles, used the pass shot effectively.

The Whites' skip used at least nine different types of strategy ends in the game. He moved the opponent around to many areas of the ice and forced him to try many different shots. He gave the opposition enormous difficulty in their shots.

It comes down to this: how many quality shots can you make, and on the final shot of the game, how much quality can you put into one shot? Not enough, so the Whites won.

The Whites' skip may appear to be a bit of a strategic genius. But he had plenty of help. First of all, he had players who could hit well (on takeout or bumper weight), draw well (guards, come arounds, freezes, backring tap backs) and position rocks well (obviously experienced sweepers). All this talent in front of him allowed excellent execution and afforded him the opportunity to call anything, particularly the right shot at the appropriate time. Had he skipped the game he did without the horses in front of him, he would have been defeated by the muscle of his opponents.

Curling is definitely a team game. All the best strategy in the world isn't worth a tinker's damn without the quality shots and the high percentage shooting team.

This hypothetical game offers a few valuable lessons for the curler. Learn about strategy from the games you play. Don't over-experiment so much that you give games away. Practise all the shots during your practice sessions so that you can skip a variety of ends in a game.

Learn to take a position in the game. For example select the finish of end six as your position end. You might be four up, two up, even, one down, three down, etc. Don't be a team that can only win from being in front on the score board. No matter how good you are, there are times when it won't go well for six ends and you need to pull it out of the fire. Learn to win from up or down and then you are a complete team.

Strategy Tips
BY RICK LANG AND AL HACKNER

The skip who says, "We'll just play and see what happens," when asked about an upcoming big game is either lying or he's missed the boat and is about to lose! Like all great golfers who play each hole in their minds before their round of golf, curlers should have an idea or game plan before the game starts.

There are three variables that might change the normal way you play the game:

1. playing conditions (ice and rocks),
2. how your opposition is playing, and
3. how your own team is playing.

If you have a set game plan, then you must also be able to alter it, depending on these three variables.

Some teams like to hit everything, some draw around everything, some teams play whatever the opposition is playing. The only answer is to play to your strengths, if you feel you are stronger, or play away from your opposition's strengths, if they happen to be good hitters, drawers, etc.

If one of the three variables forces you to play a different game, you must be able to play that game in order to be successful. Hitting teams should be able to play the draw game and draw teams, the hit. Most draw teams have to learn to be more patient. Hit teams can draw. They just have to stop panicking and stay cool, because there are six rocks in play.

How to Handle the Three Variables

1. Playing Conditions: When the rocks are bad, the percentages force you to play the hit game. When the ice is heavy at the start of the game but picks up once the pebble breaks in, then it would be wise to stay away from finesse until that point. In summary, play the finesse game only when conditions are good; when conditions are bad, be patient and hit.

2. The Opposition: When you are outgunned (playing a team that is stronger) you must gamble. Use lots of rocks in play, lots of guards and draw, draw, draw. When you are playing a weaker team, it only makes sense to keep it simple and wait for the open easy misses you know are coming.

3. Your Team: When a team member is in a slump, you must alter your game to play around him. Keep it simple until he has finished shooting. Why put pressure on your teammate when he is struggling? It is important to give him a chance to gain back his confidence.

Al Hackner, "the Ice Man."

M.B.

Mental Readiness

BY ED LUKOWICH

Are you ready? Sometimes you just have to take the bit in your teeth and go. Such a big part of sports is being ready and making your best effort.

"Be ready!" is difficult advice to explain. We demand so much of our intellect and emotions, that sometimes it's hard for us to realize whether or not we are truly ready. "Get psyched up," "bear down," "relax now," "concentrate," "let it happen," "be prepared," "don't overtrain," "get rid of the bad ones," "save a few good ones for the game," "butterflies are good," "settle down now," "turn it on," "keep cool": in all these ways we tell ourselves to do our best. We have to "psyche up," yet "stay cool" —contradictory orders. Experience has to provide the balance that allows a person to master the intellect and nerves this way.

Often we can lose our concentration and not even realize it until later. To be able to control one's inner self day in and day out is a magical feat few can manage.

Yet in reality the game begins before we ever set foot on the ice. Part of the game is won in practice, some of it is won in pregame readiness, and then the final, toughest test comes in the actual competition. This section deals with the final preparation: getting ready for the game, the shot and the situations.

To backtrack a little, let's suppose you made yourself ready for the season by working out, practising from the beginning of the year and mentally getting ready for the season. Now you are ready for competition.

I have always had a special way of getting ready for an event (bonspiel or playdown), when there have been at least seven to ten days to prepare. First, I would work out twice a day by playing squash, jogging, swimming, etc., to get physically fit to meet the practice sessions and competition ahead; these workouts were generally coupled with some positive thinking sessions—reading a book on positive thinking and outlining five or ten sayings to memorize as I worked out. (People always thought I was trying to be flexible and touch my nose to my toes, but actually I was trying to read the sayings written on the bottom of my shoes.) I find that it feels good to be in shape going into competition.

After four or five days of workouts, it was time to hit the practice ice. Sessions twice a day were the best, each lasting 45 minutes. Sometimes I'd get mad after two or three days of practice if things weren't going properly and I would throw 100 to 150 rocks in one practice session. My leg almost fell off a couple of times. But there seemed to be an adrenalin rush the last day of practice and the shots would start to flow. Mike Chernoff calls it timing (the timing of the backswing, the leg drive and the forward swing all begin to fall into place).

The two practice sessions per day closely emulated the normal two games per day of the competition.

Perhaps the greatest secret I ever had was my positive inner nature. With two games a day, I'd outline the possibilities. We could win both games, one tough, one easy; it didn't matter in what order. A game has two possible outcomes —you can win easily or squeak it out. Keep the other possibility out of your mind.

Be ready well in advance of the game so you give yourself enough time to warm up the body and the mind. You can physically warm up by stretching for five minutes before the game and then doing your practice slides and sweeping drills. But the mind needs more attention to warm up. If someone wants to gab with you or you're too complacent, mental readiness never sets in. It

The already-on-their-way team!!!

M.B.

can mean a poor start, and against a good team that can be critical.

A secret of mine is to save three positive sayings from the practice sessions. Repeat them several times and ask yourself, "Are you ready?" It's a way of demanding a mental response to action. Use those three sayings on the ice and repeat them often. A good way to stay in the game is to talk to yourself, stay on top of yourself and keep yourself focussed by running through these sayings.

The three reminders could be like these: "Okay, have a great ice-reading game, bear down on the ice reading"; or "I have the greatest draw weight in the world"; or, in pressure situations, "Don't give in to them, I'm the toughest in the world."

All these points should centre on one key thought—*make yourself forget the delivery.* Concentrate so hard on the finer points of the game that you forget the delivery, the very delivery that you worked hard on in practice, so that you can make every shot. I've used a hundred such sayings over the years and they have really helped.

A sound means of preparation is to play a few situations mentally before they occur. As a skip, expect that you will have to make one shot in the game to save it (draw against three) and visualize yourself as the hero. Expect a chance to win the game (a come-around tapout for three) and visualize yourself making it. Believe me, it will make the reality much easier if you expect it to happen.

There is also the grand act of getting ready to throw the rock. This is an art in itself. Many thousands of shots are missed in curling, as in other sports, because confusion takes over and the body and mind together "will" a missed shot.

For example, you set the broom for the shot and you're moving to play. As you hustle down the ice, doubts start to creep in. The front end players don't look really confident and your communication with them adds little or no new light. You look down at the broom and start doubting it. You doubt your ability to hit a broom that is probably in the wrong place.

You swing, and fire and concentration are lost as you release in a hurry and try to judge the stone before you have even let it go. It's so easy for your mind to bend your arm into missing the shot. Doubt is a strong force, for it can either suck the miss into itself or scare it off in a totally opposite direction. If you're deadly afraid, for instance, that the stone when released will curl too much for the required shot, you may flip it wide and miss wide. You would have been okay if you simply split the broom, but no.

To defeat this entire scenario you require a temperament that can perform under pressure. Even the best players need to work on this. When you prepare to throw the stone, the ideal attitude is to:

1. Be prepared for all eventualities, with
2. Doubts removed,
3. Inner confidence,
4. Positive feedback from teammates, and
5. A daring spirit.

Let's examine the secrets within each category that can help to make you as ready as you can be to make the shot.

1. Prepare yourself for any type of shot. Often it looks as if you will have an easy shot and all of a sudden—whammo, you have to make a dandy. It's easier if you take this attitude: "I hope he makes his shot and then I will do it better." Prepare for the toughest situation.

2. It's easy to remove doubts if you use this system. (a) Discuss the shot with your third; (b) set up a signal between yourself and the front end in case anyone feels a team discussion is necessary on the shot; (c) measure and discuss the turn and ice with your third; (d) if there are doubts, return to your first reaction (learn to have a first reaction every time their rock stops, because that's your inner experience talking to you); (e) sometimes go down the ice backwards and

M.B.

"Ready or not, here I am!"—Marilyn Darte, 1986 World Ladies' Champion.

memorize the exact location of rocks to remove confusion from your mind. Know where everything is before you settle in to concentrate on the broom. Your mind is a computer and likes to know definite locations of objects.

3. Make *one* positive statement about the shot as you approach the hack; stand tall and look confident. The body tells as much about your confidence as your words do.

4. Let the front end players hear your view on the shot and let them give you positive feedback. It's a great boost when someone expresses their confidence in what you are doing.

5. Be daring—it's easy. Don't be afraid to hit the broom and throw the rock with a feel for the shot. Let your inner self take over and let the ability flow. If you don't do that, quality shots won't happen. Let your ability and experience loose to produce quality.

Practise these methods of throwing a rock. Make it second nature and you will have overcome your greatest opponent in the game—yourself.

Section 3
Winning Methods

Fast Eddie, John Ferguson, Neil Houston and Brent Syme.   A.W.

Analyzing Positions

The Lead

In reading through the section on strategy, you will notice that every end has two main shots described: the lead's first stone and the skip's last rock. The skip's last rock is perhaps the most important shot, because it is the last chance to score or save the end. However, the lead's first stone sets the strategy for the end. If that rock is missed or out of position, your plan for the end must quickly change. Such changes do not allow the skip to *control* the strategy of the game.

Thus, the lead in today's curling has to understand strategy and the importance of proper positioning of the shots. Your draw weight has to be as good as the skip's and you must be quick to pick up changes in the ice conditions. This is critical in being able to have draw weight so that you can play exact weight shots, such as guards (centre and corner, long or short), defensive draws to the top of the four-foot (for the bumper weight in the house game), tap back shots to the back ring (to build a wall or pocket) and freezes and come-arounds, to build an end.

As well, the lead should have good hitting ability, in peel weight, regular takeout and bumper weight shots. Other attributes include

M.B.

A strong team puts all its concentration into the lead's shots—Brent Syme at work.

sweeping ability, judging weight, communicating weight and reading ice.

What you need is an individual who could probably play any other position on the team, because of ability, but prefers to play lead and is happy with the position. Usually this is a very unselfish person and a great team player.

You are fortunate if you can find and keep such a person on the team. He will certainly help your team control the strategy of the match. All you need now are three good players behind him who can maintain control and win the end. Simple, isn't it?

The Second

Several years ago, to be a top-notch team the third had to be able to make all kinds of skip's shots. Now, the second is also that kind of player. To have a good year, you have to win the majority of shootouts at the second's post; then, your third guards or puts in the extra offensive shot. You generally have to come out of second in the advantage or you may not be able to win your share of games.

If the lead is capable of setting the correct strategy for the end, the second is an instant force in gaining the advantage during it. Every shot in the book (freezes, come-arounds, taps, guards, raises, doubles) is required from this player. Thus, you need excellent shooting. Your second, like the lead, should also be a strong sweeper and a good judge of weight.

You're fortunate if one or both of the front-end players can judge weight well and take the burden away from the skip and third. This allows the top-end players to judge rocks more for the line than the weight.

Ideally one of the front end players will be a calming influence, while the other is a player with excitement and drive, to get everyone up for the game and keep them awake and alert during the match.

Front end players have the large task of keeping track of draw weight. This can be done

Neil Houston in action—the second needs all the shots of a third or skip.

M.B.

Third man Fergie was in the hospital getting his appendix out. When asked about his operation he replied, "They operated on my right hand, so I decided to get my outturn fixed as well." Woody, the second, answered, "Good, now all we have to do is get our skip to have a lobotomy and we're all set."

The third is a communication link between the skip and the front end. The third spends more time than any other player on the team talking to the skip. He can pass on tidbits of information about shots, positioning of rocks and strategy for the front end, and he also carries messages from the front end to the skip.

According to the rules of the game about players' positioning on the ice, thirds can spend time with the sweepers (they can also stand behind the house with the skip). Thirds spend a lot of time at both ends of the ice, and for this reason they are the communication link.

with a stopwatch. The third and skip are busier on strategy, ice reading and calling the sweep, so the front end should take it upon themselves to be the masters of the weight and to set up a good system for communicating this weight to the third and skip. It's all part of team play.

The Third

Thirds can make or break a team. All the skills which the skip must possess should also be found in the third. The third must be as good as the skip and he should have experience at the skip's shots as well: drawing, hitting, doubles, rolls, freezes, raises, strategy, ice reading and judging.

Another quality found on the best teams is the third's understanding of the skip. The third controls many of the ideas that crop into the skip's head. A good third knows his skip's personality and understands how to handle his skip to get the very best performance out of him. This comes from playing together and understanding one another.

M.B.

A strong third can play all the tough shots. If he is consistent, the skip is relieved of some pressure. Shown here is Rick Lang, third for Al Hackner.

Our fortunes aren't good, we fail to qualify. While waiting for our flight, some egghead suggests killing time by playing a game of billiards. So, down to the local pool hall. I am still fuming from the curling game and pool has never been my strong suit. We're playing a game called golf and if you're the first to get your ball down, it's great, but if you're the last, it's frustrating. Well, I'm last down every time. Finally I can stand no more. I fire down my cue and stomp out. Mike Chernoff turns: "So you want to be a skip, eh!"

The ad read: FOR SALE, SKIP'S BRAIN, RARELY USED, $100.

Skip

You can say the skip is all things to his team. He's the shooter, strategist, judge and ice reader. He is comparable to the scorer in hockey, who must convert the opportunities into points or else people will get tired of setting him up. He must also be like the goalie, the last line of defence, the one who must save the game in a troublesome situation.

To get the very best from his players, the skip needs to read ice extremely well. He must know his players and know how to broom them for the best results. He has to be able to pick the other team apart. He is field general (calling the right play) and a "feel player" (with the gentle touch of

Uniroyal skips pose at 1986 World Junior Championship. Front row, left to right: Scott Brown (U.S.A.), Lionel Tournier (France), Stefano Ferronto (Italy), Dieter Kolb (Germany), Markus Eggler (Switzerland). Back row, left to right: Kevin Martin (Canada), David Aitken (Scotland), Bjoern Ulshagen (Norway), Orjan Erixon (Sweden), Jorgen Larsen (Denmark).

a golf pro), a leader capable of leading by example. He should have a strong desire to be the hero, yet be capable of bouncing back when he is the goat. He must be a player capable of pulling off some circus shots. Under pressure, his eyes need the concentration of the tiger's.

A skip can win or lose the game by many means: in shooting, ice reading, brooming his players, strategy, calling the sweep and making critical decisions. Ice reading, brooming your players and being cat-like sharp on the line and weight calls have become more important for the skip each year. This is becoming a skip's best way to win the game. Anyone might shoot as well as you, but can the other skip handle the other elements too? It's a very overlooked and unpractised part of the game.

A good skip understands his players and their idiosyncrasies and can bring out the best in them. Like a teacher, the skip promotes learning and improvement in himself and his team. It is his job to give direction to this learning, helping the team to set up systems of play and ensuring that they play as a unit.

Often a skip will be out of position. The following is a list of positioning errors that as the skip, you should correct:

1. Running out to sweep—you should only do this on rare occasions and only for the last five or 10 feet when the line becomes noncritical. The skip should stay at home and read the ice.

2. Moving to sweep a roll on a takeout—leave that part up to the front end players. Complete the call and stay in position to call the hit right to the last second.

3. Standing back talking to the third when your turn to play is next—you should leave the third and move to concentrate on playing next yourself. These are vital seconds for preparing yourself to play and to be aware of the "first reaction," the one that will help you to make skipping decisions, once the other team's stone has stopped.

Coaches have become an instrumental part of the team at the Canadian and world level. Coach Joyce McKee advises her Saskatchewan team during a game's break.

Coach Alex Torrance discusses strategy with his Scottish lads. Left to right, David Smith, Torrance, Hammy McMillan, Peter Smith and Mike Hay—1986 World Men's finalists.

How to Get the Best out of Four Team Players

Number one, you want to win. But you want to have plenty of fun as well. It's not fun for the four players to play the same positions in every game all year long, regardless of whether it's 80 games or 160 games in a season. It's more interesting to switch and it also improves the team's overall skill. In today's game you need four good players, all of them capable of making every type of shot and many finesse shots. You can't have that if the lead plays nothing but lead all year long.

Set up your A team—that's your top-flight bonspiel and playoff team with everyone in position from lead to skip. Use this line-up in all the serious outings.

Set up your B team—that's everyone in the same position, but the skip throws third and the third throws skip. The skip still calls the game. This allows the third to play skip shots (you want

him to make every shot a skip will have to make). It also allows the third to be prepared if the skip can't make a game. Use this line-up in small bonspiels.

Set up your C team—that's everyone playing anywhere. Usually the skip throws lead, and the others exchange positions from game to game. The lead and second have the opportunity to throw third and skip shots. The skip still calls the game. (This is vital to success. It keeps the skipping consistent and allows the skip to continue the growth of the strategy of the team, while he practises the ice reading and the proper brooming of each player).

All the players will improve their finesse shooting and have fun with the game. It also gives each player a chance to be with the skip on the tee line and see why they are using a certain strategy. Keep the skip in the rings, that's where he can do the least damage—and on the serious side, he has to learn to have "a great game in the house" if the team is to be successful. Use this line-up in schedule games.

At times it might be advisable to let someone other than the skip call the game, as this may introduce some freshness into the strategy. Sometimes a skip gets tired of calling the same dumb shots and everyone gets tired of throwing the same dumb shots.

Improving Your Attitude

Control

In every sport, there is much written and spoken about control. Curling is no exception. When you sit into the hack and you throw a rock you want to be able to control the movement of that rock in your delivery and also control your body —you want to be able to come up with a slide that is precise, functional and consistent. To do this takes a tremendous amount of practice, and the people who are more successful practise enough so that they have excellent feel and control of their bodies during the delivery.

But control is also used in other areas of curling. It is certainly used in strategy. When you get into the game you want to be able to control the strategy. You want to feel as if the other team is playing into your hands and that you are drawing when you wish to draw, that you are playing the hitting game when you wish to play the hitting game. You have to set the trap for the other team. Although they may feel that they are doing the right thing, you must convince yourself that your ability in the long run is going to allow you to win that end. In this way, you are controlling the pace and the strategy—and in the long run, the score and the final outcome of the game.

Another area in curling that is very important

Character Builders

Forget your misses immediately. Put your energy into the next shot.

After every miss take the attitude that you are still the best. It has worked for Lee Trevino.

Whenever you miss, keep telling yourself that you are the greatest shooter in the world. Hold this belief above all others in the game.

Use the persistence principle. Keep at it and eventually you will succeed.

Take a position in the game after six or seven ends. Learn to win from various score positions. Don't be only a front runner.

Treat your team as lucky players. No head-hanging. Never feel sorry for yourself. No crutches. No easy way out. Face the music.

Don't be intimidated. Don't allow them to throw you off your game.

Always put your effort into your next shot. Don't rehash too much.

In big games, you have to keep talking to yourself. You can't turn it off and on. Talk yourself into it.

Bribe your second to say occasionally, "Have I told you lately what a great skip you are?"

Your reason for playing is to win. Play with only that one motivation. Otherwise don't bother showing up. Convince yourself the game has only one possible outcome. Lie to yourself. When you have to win, play for the great challenge.

Don't give up though the pace seems slow—
You may succeed with another blow.

Often the struggler has given up
When he might have captured the victor's cup;
And he learned too late when the night came down
How close he was to the golden crown.
      Success is failure
           turned inside out
      The silver tint
           of the clouds of doubt.
      So stick to the fight
           when you're hardest hit.
      It's when things seem
           worst that
           you mustn't quit.

to control is emotion. Often you want to get out there on the ice and get four or five ahead immediately. You have to be able to control your emotions. You have to be able to be patient—you might be two or three down, but rather than thinking, "Well, let's get it all back in one end," you have to rein in your emotions and tell yourself, "Let's take our time, let's pick away here."

As Ed Werenich says, "The most difficult things in curling to control are those inches between your ears." And in the preparation that is involved in a curling game, the psychological attitude is so important. It takes a fair amount of practice and self-analysis.

Before you can control circumstances out on the curling ice, you have to be able to control yourself. This also includes controlling your thinking when you are on the ice. Often if you are out of control, even slightly, stressful situations and difficult shots can trigger negative thoughts that become overwhelming. Your mind can just lose out to the situation. The person who is able to control his mind in a confident manner is the one who can assess the situation clearly, block out the negative thoughts and replace them with positive thoughts that bring positive action and a far better chance of success.

In the long run in curling, that ability to be able to control your negative thinking is perhaps the

"If you don't like it—stuff it!"

M.B.

most difficult challenge. In any sport negative thoughts want to creep into the situation and it is so much easier to give in to the negative thoughts than it is to hold on to your confidence. When you are going out there to play, the person that you have to win control over, and the mind that you have to win control over, is your own.

Confidence

This is an area of life where almost all of us can use some shoring up once in a while. There are many aids available to you and they are easily applicable to your own personality and needs.

One book that epitomizes the curler's struggle is *Second Effort*, authored by famous football coach Vince Lombardi. The curler, like Lombardi's football players, has his heart broken many times, but it is the ones who bounce back (the elastic people) who succeed at the roaring game.

Other great confidence-building books include the entire series by Dr. Norman Vincent Peale and many books on psycho-cybernetics (steering one's mind to a productive and useful goal). Cassette tapes based on the books are also available. These books teach you to work on your self-image, improve your confidence vocabulary and appear more confident.

Practise removing the "if" or "doubt" words from your vocabulary. On the ice, your actions speak loudly to your teammates. Indecision will be easy to read. When you react angrily to your small defeats, you will lose in the long run. Only one person in a million can use anger to win. There just aren't too many John McEnroes or Paul Gowsells around. When you settle into the hack, be convinced that you are the most successful person you know.

The skipper (Mr. Bia Mile) fanned his final stone. Furiously he flung his broom and shoes out the door and retreated into the washroom. There he stood over the sink with his wrists slit. His buddy walked in and asked, "Wanna skip our team in the cash?" Our skipper: "What time's our first game?" They always keep coming back for more...

United Press Canada

"Why don't you come down and fight like a man?"—Barry McPhee of Kamloops, B.C.

The Importance of Concentration

M.B.

Totally absorbed in the game—
Judy Lukowich.

Does the athlete who can concentrate the best win?

Yes, that athlete does win, but there are a few points to remember.

People with tremendous concentration are very fortunate. It is a gift, a skill that is difficult to measure. It is a form of self-hypnosis. While the mind locks in, the body is ordered to perform at its peak. Everything outside of the arena of the game is shut out. The match becomes the world, the great escape from reality, two to three hours of absorbing mental punishment. The amount of concentration a person can bring to a match is in direct proportion to his desire to play that match. If you are hungrier than a hound dog and this match is the biggest thing in your universe, then tremendous concentration is possible. If the reason for playing is to pick up an easy victory but you'd rather be somewhere else, then concentration is very difficult. It's the player who wants to win the most, who has prepared the most and who intends to bear down the most, who can exert the greatest concentration.

Can you turn your concentration on and off? You can turn it off only slightly. In a game, that would be a light moment of talking to the opposing players or taking a break for a laugh or two; however, the mind never really loses concentration and when asked to pay attention, it can readily do so.

You need to give yourself pep talks during the game and keep your concentration active. Al Hackner's 1982 world's team used to call a lapse in concentration "a trip to the Barbados." It is often caused by boredom: too many games, too many of the same dumb shots, just a tired mind. You have to bear down for ten full ends and breaks in your concentration must be minor. Then it's back to full gear.

Early in the year, practise tunnel vision during a game. Pretend there is a long tent covering your sheet and no other activities or games are going on around you. Your game is the only one in town.

After that game, run through a mental checklist. Did you know the scores from other games? Did you see other deliveries and shots on other sheets? If you concentrated hard you only saw your own game.

Later in the year you may learn to curl with tunnel vision and only glance at something else intentionally. This technique will relieve pressure and give you a break. It will not make you lose concentration. It is a way to ease tension so you can step outside yourself for a second.

A.W.

This player's eyes are fixed on the broom at the far end—Judy again.

M.B.

The Key Shots: Drawing and Hitting

"Ninety per cent of the rocks hogged never end up counting" —Confucius says.

Okay, so you have to get the stone over the hog line. But how can you get to make more shots? First of all, you can practise more. Also, you can develop a better understanding of the shots and the best techniques to use in executing them.

Let's first pretend that all the shots are simple draw or takeout. Is there a difference in the delivery for these two shots? Most players throw the same delivery for a takeout or a draw and they

play very well. However, some players who slide out low are great on takeouts, and not quite as good on drawing. Others have a fine draw delivery, but can't seem to hit accurately. Is there a reason for this?

There is probably not a delivery in existence that is completely as good for takeout as it is for draw, or vice versa. This does not imply that you should throw your delivery away or change it drastically. But understanding some of the reasons for this statement may give you a tip on making a successful change or addition to your style.

The hitting slide is low—the body is extended.

M.B.

As Ed Werenich shows, the draw slide is higher and the front leg and arm do not stretch out as much towards the broom.

M.B.

Let's compare hitting and drawing.

Hitting
• The arm is extended to the target.
• The best hitting deliveries have a lower slide with the stone placed out front.
• The speed of the slide is direct and forceful with a strong leg-drive.
• The sliding foot reaches out towards the target.
• The slide foot turns sideways more, to facilitate the low slide and the extended sliding leg.
• The body weight is on the flat foot and the body stays back.

Exception: Toe sliders may not show much difference in hit or draw delivery, but they do tend to extend more for takeouts than draws.

Drawing
• The rock is not extended in front of the body as much, but sits back a little in a "sweet spot." The arm has a slight bend to feel the weight.
• The speed of the delivery is slower with the weight coming more from the stone and less from the leg drive.
• The sliding foot is under the abdomen more than the chest, and the foot is not turned as much.
• The slide does not get much lower towards the release, whereas the hitter gets lower on the release.
• The body weight may start on the flat foot but at release it is slightly more on the toe. The heel may come up slightly, because the foot is back a little further.

Just as a golfer can play many shots (hook, slice, drive, chip), a curler can use various techniques to enhance the execution of a shot. If you don't already have the best of both worlds (good takeout and good draw), perhaps you should consider using more than one type of delivery in your style.

These techniques may vary only slightly for hits and draws and the normal spectator may not even notice a difference. But the feeling of accuracy or weight may improve a great deal by the change. Experiment with your delivery (if you have a weakness) and see if the strengths outlined on hitting and drawing work for you.

Tips on Playing the Shots: Draw, Guard, Freeze
Keep track of only one weight. It occurred to me one day that I always had a great feel for back ring weight (sort of like the ball player with warning track power). Thus, I decided to use back ring weight as the basis for my personal

The "slider" on the sliding shoe should be fast enough that it does not stick even a tiny bit on ice when the pebble is wearing off. But it should not be so fast that the player loses the feel of the ice for draw weight. the best draw players prefer a medium-speed slider.

M.B.

weight system, rather than tee weight.

I'd observed very closely the way rocks stopped (the last five feet before the rock stops tells you plenty about the feel for that spot). Advice from the front end and their stopwatch might indicate 12 seconds draw weight, as an example. Because I always had a great feel for back ring weight, it seemed to be the easiest weight for me to throw consistently on any type of ice; I'd slide out with the back ring weight for a draw and I'd pretend I was throwing the stone into the rings from the last hog line (this made it seem simple). Then I'd toss it to the top of the eight-foot and let the sweepers have it.

This helped my draw weight greatly because my delivery did not have a push. I was in trouble if I came out too slowly, the rock had no momen-

tum. Now I always came out fast enough and just felt the weight. At least I always came out with the speed of a back ring draw on all draws and guards; not one time a guard, another tee line, another top of the house. This change made my draw weight far more consistent.

Remember to rely more on your feel than on the stopwatch or advice. Feel is your experience flowing out, your natural talent coming through. You can't touch or box or take a picture of "feel." But you sure can destroy it in a hurry by not letting it out. Your body, because it has played the game before, naturally responds to it, and if not forbidden from doing so it can probably produce the correct amount of "feel." But overthinking, doubts and tightness can keep it down. Often a player asks, "What is draw weight?" If you can successfully lie to them and say, "Don't worry, you've got it, so make the shot!", they will do just that. React! Don't think! Let your body observe and react naturally. There is a time and a place to tell your brain to get out of the way.

With draws, use this scale as a guide to the amount of sweeping you should use throughout the game. Throw more to your sweeping as the game goes on.

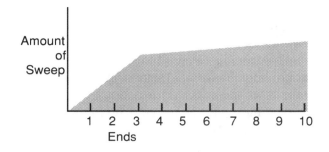

Hitting: Takeouts, Bumpers, Peels
Use more leg drive and the "one thought principle." Evaluate your weight and back swing ahead of time and then concentrate on the broom only. Forget the weight. Feel will take care of that. Concentrate your eyes on the bottom of the broom and see nothing else.

Don't be afraid to hit the broom. It's there for a reason. If you're afraid to be wide you'll be narrow, and vice versa.

To play high percentage on hits, learn to throw them into sweep. Throw the rock intentionally into sweep. The shot is either on the broom or a half-inch inside. It's called a controlled release. Once you are hitting the broom well, it's a fine way to play your hits.

Back Ring Shots and Hack Weight Shots

Play these off draw weight. These critical shots should not be overthrown so don't use takeout weight as your base but rather draw weight and then add the necessary amount of weight.

With all the shots, play only in one sphere. Throw the rock for only one reason—to make it. It's so simple. The shots are so easy. It's only our overactive minds that make them difficult.

Every Shot in the Book

Many experienced players still don't play the right weight for the shot. Here is an example: a possible double of A and B.

Takeout weight was thrown, and A was hit two-thirds and removed, with the shooter rolling across the face of B. The opponent now has an easy shot. Sure, the double was possible, but the weight was wrong. Play a required weight that can't roll out. Easy board (bumper) weight would make the double as A is struck two-thirds, or would make the roll freeze if A is struck one inch thicker. Either shot is great.

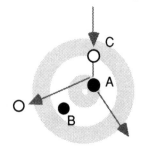

Let's look at all the possible weights to be used to take out A and B.

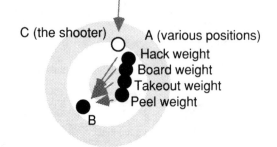

The principle is simple. Get the double, but if you can't, save the shooter. Far too many skips don't know how to save the shooter. Learn to play the same shot with different weight and learn to play doubles with something more than just takeout or peel weight.

Raises

Raises are fun shots. They are game breakers. However, if the opponent still has a shot left *keep track of the shooter*. You might make a great raise, but will your raised stone be guarded? Think of the shooter's roll before the shot and perhaps that will dictate your weight as well.

The High, Hard One

The high, hard takeout shot in curling is one that is used very, very little, one that very few curlers can throw accurately and also one that very few curlers ever practise. It certainly is a handy shot to have around and quite often at the end of a practice, it's good to throw one or two of them just to test them out. The weight for the shot can be determined by a number system. Here is one type of number system you could use: suppose there is regular takeout, around a six and your peel weight is around seven; when you jump from six to seven you are increasing your weight 10 to 15 feet or thereabouts.

Now the high, hard one can be broken down into a number division. Use two numbers, an 8 and a 10. The 8 is again another 10 to 15 harder than the peel shot; and there is one even higher than that (which would be around a 10) that is a further 10 or 15 feet harder. The most common use of this shot is in situations where you are doing a jump shot, where the angle is very difficult and you have to hit a lot of the rock you are shooting at and jump almost straight across with your shooter. It is often used for those very difficult doubles or triples that can crop up in the game. The shot could be overused to the point where it could be a drawback to your play—you certainly don't want to use the shot unless your chances of making it are very, very high. It is a shot that has to be practised.

In practising the shot, remember that it is simply a slightly higher backswing than you normally would use, and a much earlier release. In the shot that you usually use for a peel shot, you have a good backswing and good timing. Then you come out and you let your peel shot go normally, somewhere past the house or the rings.

With the high hard one, you increase your backswing ever so slightly—still trying to maintain good timing—and let the rock go in the rings. The shot described as a 7 or an 8 is released pretty close to the end of the rings, whereas a high, hard shot would be released somewhere before the T line or just around the T line.

If you are required to let go of a rock sooner than that, it is very difficult to guarantee your accuracy. Because it is released early, the rock is thrown without much steering involved. It's really just a clean release shot. It is a great shot to practise because it tells you a lot about your delivery; it's good to throw it once or twice per practice because it may help you to straighten out your normal slide. Since it is essentially just a swing and a release, it is a true indicator of what

High and higher—Bob Pickering, curling's highest backswing.

your backswing and your downswing are like.

In practice, start out with a good swing and let the rock go right from the hack. That will tell you where you are setting the rock down. Just let the rock go, don't try to steer. This will show you where your backswing is at the top. It will also be a perfect indicator of where your downswing is when the rock is in the first few feet of the ice. As discussed throughout this book, a key point of the curling delivery is, "Where is the rock in the downswing and in the first few feet of the slide?" This shot will give you the answer, and it is a reliable guidance system.

By practising the shot more, you will slowly —just by trying to throw at a broom with a very early release—develop a downswing that is in a better position in the first few feet of the slide. Keep practising, and you will find that you will be able to throw a high, hard one quite accurately. It will help out your normal delivery as well.

In a good delivery, the player is invariably in an exceptionally good spot with the curling rock in the first few feet of the slide or the very, very end of the downswing. When a player is off line at that point in his delivery, you can be sure that he is going to be doing some funny things with the curling rock before he finally releases it. Even though he may tend to make a lot of shots and get it back on line, you can start to use strategy against him. The rock from that point has to be angled or released oddly on certain types of shots or when the broom is in a certain place. A good strategist will take advantage of that weakness and will immediately start to play particular shots. These shots will force the thrower to throw into areas where his delivery or release become difficult and work against him.

A word of caution about the high, hard shot. Do not play it because it is spectacular or because you are looking to impress, or because there is a big crowd and you want to show off. Throw it because it is the logical shot at a particular time. It is *always* a gamble shot because it is thrown hard and it can always be fanned. But only play it if it is a high-percentage shot and it should be played.

"Our skip is the only person who would stand in front of a micro-wave oven and yell 'hurry!'"

M.B.

Another word of warning is in order about the high, hard shot. It is best for this shot to be thrown into sweeping. Do not take much ice. Always take ice on the rock that you are aiming at. The shot is thrown either on the broom or one or two inches inside. That is where your target is. Often the rock will even run back when it is thrown that hard, so take narrow ice, throw it on the broom or an inch or two inside and let it run. Certainly do not throw it into space if there is a chance to fan everything.

Always be sure that your team knows when a high, hard rock is being thrown, because there is nothing worse than the rock sailing by the sweepers when they are not alert, and they are not there to sweep. A sweeper should be with the rock, to sweep it when it is needed. The sweepers on a hard, high one need to start a little further back and get a good run so that they can be moving with the rock.

Sweeping on this shot can be very important. Just touching it once or twice down the ice at the right point can make a difference, and there are some high, hard rocks that actually curl because they hit a certain speed. They may even curl, at times, more than a regular takeout. This only happens when they are thrown exceptionally hard. It probably occurs because they are moving very fast and creating a bit of a vacuum.

It takes a good athlete to be able to run and sweep one of these rocks, so be prepared.

M.B.

Sweeping and Calling

Sweeping and calling of the shot as it travels its path down the ice are combined in this section because they are closely related. The two skills work hand in hand in the seconds the stone takes to travel from release to target. Sometimes the caller is in charge and other times the sweeper. Let's examine the techniques of sweeping and calling.

Cleaning the Ice before the Shot

Let's suppose the game has just completed an end at the B rings. The ice is likely to be very clean from hack A to the hog line A, as that was kept clean for all the released shots from that end. If there is debris on the ice, and there certainly

To be in control the players must work as a unit. Here are Mike Riley (sliding), Russ Wookey (left sweeper), John Helston (right sweeper) and Brian Toews (third), 1984 Canadian Brier winners.

will be if straw (corn) brooms were used, the majority of it will be between hog A and the back of rings B.

We will play from hacks at B and throw back through all that debris. So clean the line from hack B to five feet past hog B to allow the lead player a clean delivery. (If the other team is to play first, don't clean the line until it is your turn. If they aren't smart enough to do it, that's their problem.)

Do not, once your turn to play has come, clean the ice before the shot from hog B to the A rings. Your normal sweeping and cleaning of the path of the stone as it travels will take care of this. In particular, if there is straw from hog A to rings A, it may help you to position your shot.

If you are playing against strong corn broom sweepers, mentally keep track of debris. For instance, in the illustrations shown here, a stone travelled along the path and was swept hard most of the way. If you play down that same path, the ice will likely be relatively clean. The opposite side of the ice, however, probably will have caught all the straw debris and will be a heavier path. Notice where the straw is and be very careful of corn broom sweepers who are overly nice and clean the path for you when it is no longer their shot. They are trying to trap you into a keen spot that does not pick up any of the normal debris that will slow the shot down appropriately.

Positioning

The photo above is an ideal illustration of proper technique. The thrower is down and following through on takeout, and up and chasing close on draws. The sweepers are with the stone from start to finish and they give the callers a perfectly clear view. Their feet are to the side and the brush handles are not over the rock.

The heads are in perfect position to view the path far ahead, to detect signals from the rings, to view 10 feet in front of the stone for debris and to glance down at the stone occasionally to see its speed.

The person in the rings is low for hits, and up high for straight draws to see the weight better. He is up and down on draws around guards to see both the curl and the weight interchangeably. The person in the rings stays "at home" and does not come out to sweep except if called upon by the sweepers on a straight draw shot.

The thrower never sweeps and is always there as the final judge, should the person in the rings run out at the last second to help out around guards. On takeouts, the person in the rings stays down to complete the calls and the sweepers are alert to sweep rolls, doubles and other rocks set in motion.

The Caller's Vocabulary

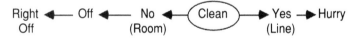

Right Off ← Off ← No (Room) ← Clean → Yes (Line) → Hurry

These are one-word commands. With good throwers, the most common word is "clean" (or nothing is said at all) if the sweepers are nursing the stone properly. The call "room" is often substituted for the call "no" if the reason for not sweeping is that there is too much room by a guard and the stone needs to curl.

"Line" is substituted for "yes" if you are playing a guard too tight. Be very careful in calling "off" or "right off" against straw. Rocks will pick up debris and suddenly curl too far. A better call is a soft "no" with one person cleaning. If there is straw on the ice, you can get

"right off" the rock 10-20 feet later and usually still get plenty of curl. Yelling "right off" too early is a mistake that inexperienced players make against straw teams.

The Sweeper's Vocabulary

The calls are to let the thrower and particularly the person in the rings know about the weight. The vocabulary is: weight; heavy or light on takeouts; depth of draws; back ring, tee, front ring, light, etc.; hack weight shots; at the final hog, is there enough weight to tap the stone out of the rings.

Sweeper's Duties

These are listed here in order of importance. Always know the particular path for curl and weight.

Takeout	Draw	Hack Weight
1. React 2. React while calling the weight. 3. React while remembering the spot. For example, in straight spot use only one sweeper till the second "yes" is called.	1. Judge the weight. 2. Judge the weight while yelling the weight. 3. React to line calls.	1. Seventy-five per cent react to call. Twenty-five per cent judge the weight. 2. Communicate the weight.

Communication between the Sweepers and the Caller

Try to keep the central theme of your calling as "clean" if you play on a team of good throwers. The less you allow yourself to jump to calls such as "hurry" or "off," the more effective you'll be. The key is, when a rock is well thrown, know how to keep it clean and properly nurse it down the ice.

Four Elements of Sweeping

1. Power or speed
2. Judging
3. Reacting
4. Communicating

Before the rock is thrown, while the line between the hack and 10 feet past the hog is briefly cleaned, the sweeper should determine his duty. If the shot is a line shot (takeout), the main duties are to listen and react.

Reaction is so important. Staying on or off the rock for an extra five feet against the calling can ruin the best shot, as well as hurt the calling system for future shots. The number one rule is to react on hits. Only call the weight if it's definitely wrong. The sweeper should understand that the call "clean" means to keep the line clean with very soft stroking, while allowing for normal curl.

A.W.

It's best to learn to sweep with both types of broom. It gives your game more style! Pamela Lukowich is the model.

M.B.

The corn broom roars back.

On straight draws the sweeper becomes judge and communicator and reactor, in that order. On tight come-arounds, with draw or hack weight, the duties are to react first to the calls, and supplement this with communicating and judging.

Brushes and Brooms

Till 1975, corn brooms and synthetic brooms were mostly used in sweeping. As early as 1965, John Mayer of Calgary picked up the idea of brushes from a Scottish team touring Canada. John made his own brushes. As a matter of fact he used angle brushes as well back then. He played lead on the Bruce Stewart team from Calgary and soon their entire team used them. They curled out of the Winter Club and gradually a few others there began to use them too. The team was successful, but everyone laughed at the brushes and maintained that they would never use them. Paul Gowsell of the same club, however, began using it in Junior curling. Then

brooms in use. Today the brush remains dominant but there are many teams still using corn brooms. They find that the corn broom is more exercise for the arms and it adds more action to the game. It puts debris on the ice and lends a better curl for the draw game. Both types of brooms are excellent and some teams like to use both.

The power (of the Canadians) and the speed (of the Europeans) in brushing are terrific and both are effective. Power is best on hard pebble to break it down. Speed is efficient on keen ice.

Always use a proper cleaning system when you are brushing, especially against straw. Be sure to leave room for the rock to move considerably in the last 30 feet. On clean ice, the biggest error is oversweeping. Jumping all over a rock can wreck a closely thrown shot that needed either "clean" or "moderate" sweep.

M.B.

Al Hackner displays proper positioning by following close behind his draw, acting as the judge.

An obvious error is four people out sweeping and no one left calling the line.

M.B.

"Harder!!!" —Neil Harrison and John Kawaja.

in 1976, Paul won his first Junior World Curling title. For two or three years thereafter, he controlled the winning board in major cashspiels.

In 1978 Ed Lukowich and his team from Medicine Hat began using the brush and at the 1978 Brier at Vancouver they were the first team ever to curl in the Brier with brushes. They won. By 1979 more than half the teams at the Brier had brushes and by 1980 there were hardly any straw

Western curlers have always used a bag of tricks for sweeping. They keep a few new corn brooms in the team bag and break them out if the game is going badly. They begin using them to put debris on the ice, thus changing the playing surface. The opposition, they hope, will be too inexperienced to call and sweep on the new surface. This is a common practice in Western Canada, due to the longtime use of the inverted (big-ended straw) straw brooms that break on the

Here is an example of excellent use of arms and wrists—Jeff Thomas and his Newfoundland mates.

M.B.

M.B.

Stay low (photo at left) to call the line. Use your hands if there is too much noise. Use one-word commands. Once you have the line (photo above), stay up high to get the best judgement of the weight and help the sweepers with the weight of the draw.

Tommy "Groovey" Wilson was famous for his powerful rink-rat sweeping technique and especially for his tenacity in never giving up on a rock. In one game he was sweeping a draw into the rings with nothing else in play and the opposing skip was walking up to lay the broom for the hit. The unsuspecting skip, seeing the rock stop, stepped forward, but "the Ungroove" wasn't done. With his last swipe he caught the skip in the ankle with his powerful rink-rat and knocked him right on his bum. What the skip didn't realize was that Tom did and still does hold the world's record for the most minutes swept after the rock has stopped.

straw ends and leave plenty of debris on the ice. Eastern Canada outlawed the inverted straw and the problem has been eased.

Our own team loves to play against straw and really enjoys seeing the other team break out new corn. We sweep well against it and use the corn to our advantage. We do not spend any extra minutes cleaning it off the ice ahead of time. We keep track of where it is and we can benefit from it. We consider it the first admission of defeat when the other team brings it out. In 1983 we stopped carrying new corn in our bags, since we consider it a crutch that we don't want when we head onto the ice. Either we beat the other team straight up or it's bar time.

M.B.

Coping with Pressure

Anxiety and Performance

BY EUGENE HRITZUK AND ED LUKOWICH

One of the greatest factors in the top performance of a curler is a state of psychological readiness that results in optimum performance. If a curler is not emotionally ready or "up" for a game, performance suffers. On the other hand, if a curler is over-anxious, performance can also be impaired. The relationship between anxiety and performance is shown in the diagram at right.

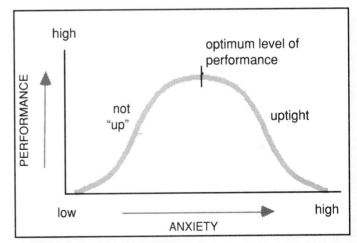

This bell-shaped curve applies to many players. They perform better as they concentrate harder and get more keyed up. However, if they get too nervous and uptight, it's like a spring giving way. Their performance drops right off. Pressure forces their level of anxiety too high and their normal physical skills fall apart, damaging their performance.

A typical example happens in pro golf, where the player leading may carry all the pressure on his shoulders for three days and finally play badly on the fourth day. The other players are coasting along, playing without the pressure, and they play exceptionally well on the final day.

Another example happens on the curling ice on a big shot late in the game. As pressure mounts, the player tends to freeze up.

It pays to get psyched up for the game and welcome the pressure of the big match but as the tension of the game builds higher and higher, use secrets to relax yourself and your teammates.

As the great Ernie Richardson once theorized, "A team's success is directly related to their ability to handle mounting pressure, and that can be best accomplished by a belief in one another." That is the key—to believe in one another.

It makes it so much easier when you have people around who believe in you and in return you have to show respect and belief in their abilities. But you can't demand belief from people. You have to earn it by your actions and your abilities and your response to pressure.

The following article by Warren Hansen describes perhaps the greatest pressure shot ever in a Brier, in which a skip earned the belief of his team and the country.

Champ Used Long Guard as a Precise Guideline

Even though The Shot was made a while ago, at the Labatt Brier in Moncton, 1985, curlers are still talking of Al Hackner's tenth-end double

which gave his Northern Ontario team a game tying deuce in the final against Pat Ryan of Alberta.

When Ryan trotted to the hack for his last shot of the tenth, leading by two, Alberta was sitting shot at roughly 6:30 in the eight-foot ring and the rock was hidden by a Northern Ontario second-shot at 11:30 in the 12-foot. In addition, Hackner owned a biter at 2:30 and a long guard covering the eight-foot to the same side of the rings (fig. 1).

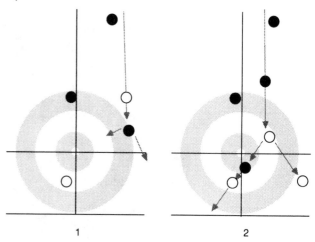

Ryan elected an outside-in kill on the Hackner biter with a roll to the inside behind the long guard. Yet there are those who argue that had Ryan passed on his shot, Hackner would have been more hard pressed to find a shot that would have netted him a pair.

However, Ryan's decision was based on eliminating opposing stones and thereby holding Hackner to no more than a tying deuce. Even after Ryan had made the shot, rolling to sit one and two, few realized a narrow opening had been left for Hackner.

It required precise passage of his last stone by the guard but Hackner chose outturn ice, delivered and made the shot perfectly (fig. 2).

As contradictory as it may appear, the presence of the guard actually aided Hackner with the shot. It acted as a guideline. Simply, with correct weight and successful narrow clearance of the guard the shot was there to be made.

Hackner's positive release technique—his rocks rarely begin to move until mid-ice—also aided in the achievement.

It was a great shot, executed by a great player under supreme pressure. And it provided a lesson to curlers everywhere.

The next time you have to play a fine shot around a guard, remember to use that guard as a guide just as Al Hackner used it so successfully.

W.H.

Where does the power come from to see the race to its end? From within.

Another curler, well known to Alberta Championships, has his own homegrown method to overcome pressure.

"Evil Roy Slade"—Roy Talbot, from Red Deer—had to execute a takeout to win and was trying to build his confidence by talking to himself on the long journey from house to hacks. "Okay, Roy, you can make it. Just think about the size of that rock. It's big as a boxcar, big as a boxcar, big as a boxcar." He reached the hack, then turned around and commented, "It looks like a pea."

A skip should spend some time with his team during the game. Most skips never do this. They talk to the third on strategy, race down to throw the stone, partly recognizing the front end, and then they throw. The rest of the time they spend behind the rings by themselves. There are times during a game when it is important to break this routine.

At the completion of an end, the skip should follow through often and consult the rest of the team about the next end. Where should the first rock be placed? What type of end should they play? If the last shot of the finished end was missed, this consultation also prevents the other three players from discussing the skip's screw-up with one another.

After a bad end, the worst thing a skip can do is stand at the far end and see those three pairs of sad eyes looking back at him. It's better to enter

M.B.

The skip should take time during every game to talk strategy with teammates—Keith Wendorf (middle) of West Germany and his team.

the fray and settle everyone down. Forget about that miss and get everyone to concentrate on the next end. Meet the pressure head on, face up to it together and don't let one individual take the brunt.

Sometimes the best way to cope with pressure situations is to convince yourself and others that you are a little reckless and cavalier. Lie to yourself and everyone else that pressure doesn't bother you.

Develop rituals to relax yourself. Get in the hack for your shot and take the time to glance at a shot on the next sheet. Spin the rock around a few times in your hand. Learn to enjoy the moment rather than dread it.

That moment of pressure can be one of life's truly great experiences, so make the most of it. I remember once when the pressure was almost getting to me. It was in the Nipawin Carspiel quarter-finals. The other team had peeled everything for five ends. We tied them on the tenth end. In the eleventh, they peeled the first six and I settled angrily into the hack to place my guard, mumbling something about not being able to get one dumb guard out there. Loudly Woody, our second man, answered, "Yeah, but it's early yet!"

The opposing skip peeled my guard and he also peeled when I put my last one on the button. We finally got a guard and stole the second extra end. Woody was right. It was early yet.

Make pressure your friend rather than your enemy. Have some fun with the big match. I can remember a time in curling when we were so serious that we wouldn't even smile, let alone laugh, when we made a bit shot. We thought it might offend the other team or make us look like jerks. Who cares! We needed to lighten up. You don't want to be an idiot on the ice. But life is far too long to have a bad time while you are out there.

A Quick Trick to Beat Stress
BY AL HACKNER

Every curler feels pressure whether he is an average club curler or the world champion. Yes, even the iceman feels pressure! But how that pressure is handled separates the winners from the losers.

First, let's examine what pressure is. Pressure is wanting to be successful and win a big game or make a big shot. Pressure is also fear of failure if you lose or miss an easy shot. You can overcome this anxiety with practice.

Here's the scene. You are playing in the biggest game of your life. You're nervous!

That's okay because you can turn that energy into a plus factor. You must do two things. First, you must slow down. There is an overwhelming tendency to rush into everything because you are excited. Mistakes are made when pressure makes you rush a shot or rush into a bad strategy call. Take your time on the shots, take a couple of extra seconds to look over the situation.

Now, you are in the hack, and you have to draw to the four-foot to win the game. A tightness comes over you. Your heart is pounding. Take a couple of deep breaths. This helps to calm you down. You must then concentrate on the shot itself, not the outcome if you miss. Think the line, think weight, picture the shot being made in your mind—then make that shot.

M.B.

André Flotron, 1984 Cornwall, Canada Uniroyal World Junior Curling Championship.

Section 4
Finer Points

Freezes

The freeze is curling's finest finesse shot. It is a combination of excellent draw weight, accurate ice reading and fine sweeping and judging—definitely a teamwork shot.

The shot is made easier than a normal draw because you have the stone to be frozen to as a guide. Yet you're trying to stop a draw shot within one or two inches of a spot, from over one hundred feet away. A team that can make many of these freezes can give the opposition shots with a higher degree of difficulty.

Here are a few hits on freezing:

1. If there is a second stone in position, let it help you with the freeze:

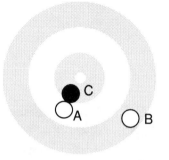

Freeze the right-hand side of the rock so that both A or B could save the freeze shot C if the opponent tries to run it out.

2. If the freeze is coming to the pro side (not curling fully up to the stone to be frozen):

a) don't bump off.

b) the bump-off splits the rocks apart.

c) better to stop 2 to 3 inches short.

3. If the freeze is going amateur (curling across the face, curling too much):

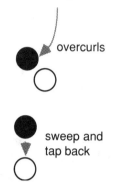

overcurls

sweep and tap back

Sweep the stone and create a slight bump. The shooter stays straighter by being swept and inertia takes some of the weight out of the soft bump. Thus the shooter is in line with the back rock.

Ever lost a game on this shot?

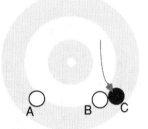

A   B   C

The opponent is lying two counters and with the last stone you will freeze to stone B to count one. (It is a poor idea to use backing for a draw, because it normally causes the thrower to be a bit heavy.) The broom is placed for a perfect draw to stone B. The weight looks a tiny bit heavy, but the line is pretty good too.

Just before the final hog, the third observes that if the stone is swept "all out" the rest of the way, it will hit B dead on and tap it back a couple of feet. This is now, in his eyes, a totally sure shot. He begins to scream "sweep!" and one sweeper reacts by sweeping while the other yells out "the weight might be okay." This sweeper feels it may stop in time and he refuses to sweep.

Now, the rock begins to overcurl slightly, the third is screaming to sweep, some are sweeping and some aren't. The rock overcurls and stops at point C for third shot. A steal of two.

M.B.

Debbie Jones (sweeping) and Linda Moore
(centre), 1985 World Ladies' Champions, take
on Marilyn Darte (centre, behind) and Kathy
McEdwards in the 1986 Canadian Ladies' final.

There is one right way to play this shot. It may
be a draw, but when the third calls hard sweeping at the last hog line and is positive of the direct
tap of the shooter onto stone B, everyone goes
with this judgement and the shot is made. Make
this unwritten rule part of your team play. A little
bit of this and a little bit of that just doesn't work
on this shot.

M.B.

"The slap shot."
Russ Howard of Ontario (centre) and Al Harnden of Northern Ontario (front right).

Ice Reading

Although the chief ice reader is the skip, all the players on the team need to observe ice. The front end players watch for trails in the ice and they use this knowledge in their sweeping. They should be equally concerned with the keen and heavy trails on the sheet, whether they use observation or stopwatch or both.

The third works both ends. He acts as a front end player in watching the ice for hints to use in sweeping, and he also keeps a sharp eye on the curl of the ice from both ends of the sheet, so he can help the skip discuss the ice and call the sweep.

The skip observes the weight of the ice as rocks stop, but he leaves most of the timing by stopwatch to the front end players. He'll time the odd shot, just to stay in touch. His main concern, however, is to read the curl of the ice.

This ice reading by the skip is very important because it affects every one of the 80 shots of the game. The quicker a skip can type or classify a sheet of ice or all the sheets in a rink, the easier the rest of the job becomes. There are some sheets that fall into a definite class: peaked (often caused by high centre tape), bowled (caused by outside pebble build-up), slanted, high centre, and high shoulders.

Once you know the pattern of the ice you can broom your players away from danger. For example, on peaked ice, keep the broom very

"Can folding your arms really improve your ice reading?"—Al (left) and Rick (right) and Dave Iverson of Manitoba (lower).

M.B.

ice to his advantage. On peaked ice, play a strong side guard game with last rock advantage. It's easy to bury shots towards the corners. Let the type of ice influence your strategy game.

Watch the running of the stone down the ice for two special points: How did the rock curl to the three-quarter pole (10 feet before final hog)? Did the rock finish (curl the last 30 feet)?

Normally rocks run straight from the release to the three-quarter pole, and curl more from the three-quarter pole to the stop point as the weight comes off the stone. Knowing how the rock will finish enables the skip to ice the shot properly and call the sweep. Measure certain spots in the ice. Keep track of how many feet and inches a rock curls.

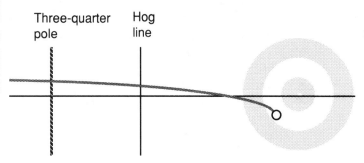

The third and skip should use this measuring technique together to discuss the ice for a shot. Recall past shots as examples for one another to help you to remember the ice.

tight on shots towards centre as the danger is wide; play all takeouts outside-in. With a rock on the centre line, choose the side where most of the rock reaches over the line. This allows you to stay away from the tricky centre. Play draws to bury across the centre without sweep. These are the only stones that will curl across centre.

You can see how the skip is using this type of

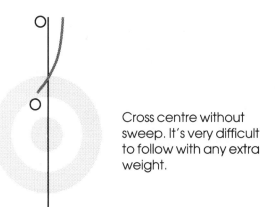

Cross centre without sweep. It's very difficult to follow with any extra weight.

Brooming Your Team

Two schools of thought are used by skips in brooming their players. School one says to read the ice the same way for all players. Give them all the same ice for similar shots. If a player tends to make a rock curl more in a spot, then that player must make an in-the-game adjustment to hit the broom properly.

This school is in fact left in the dust as too many errors can result when each player tries to make in-the-game adjustments. In this book, we refer often to "forgetting your delivery" during the game and concentrating on the shots. When a skip refuses to broom a player for a slightly different release, then the player has to resort to a delivery change during the game. That simply makes the player remember the delivery and causes too many mental errors.

School two says to read the ice slightly differently for each player. Not all players throw the same. There are different releases and righthanded players throw opposite to lefthanded players (refer to the section on delivery, p.23). Certain players release earlier (the rock curls more). Some players push the stone (it will run much straighter).

School two uses the following method. Practise the delivery and releases during the practice sessions to make them as consistent as possible. That is the key word—*consistent*. The skip should hold the broom for his players regularly in practice to see how their inturn and outturn are running. On the ice, during the game,

M.B.

"A little more ice please."

the skip should ask that each player make *no* adjustment and that he keep throwing the same release at the skip so that the skip can broom them properly.

As the skip, if your player's inturn curls a little more, give him a little more ice. As a matter of fact, have this player play inturn bury shots, as it

A skip and third work together on icing shots—Ron Mills (third) and Rick Folk (right, skip).

may be difficult for the opposition to follow. Use what the player does to your advantage. If your player's outturn is straighter, then play the ice tight and don't oversweep.

Consistency, that's what you want. It doesn't matter if a player is narrow in a certain spot for a thousand times in a row, as long as he does it every time and you can broom it properly.

This relates to my earlier statement in this book that the skip can win the game by having a great game in the house. By brooming his players and himself properly, many more shots can be made.

As for me, one week my inturns may be just a tiny bit narrow, but I do it every time. Two weeks later, that inturn may be over-corrected in practice, so that it's now always a little wide, but I continue to do it every time. So I just broom the shot properly, and leave the delivery in the locker room. Forget the delivery! Just throw the real you and broom it properly.

"Nice shot!"

A.W.

Quality Shots

One fall, one of the teams had 25 wins and no losses while playing in smaller events. Finally they entered the car bonspiel and lost three in a row, getting knocked out. They were all close tough games. But while the players were high percentage shooters, when it came to the finesse game their shots lacked a little quality.

How do you make the adjustment to play against the best teams and stick with them on the quality shots? The answer is, practise plenty and play everybody and continually improve. Work on shots such as come arounds, hack weight tapouts, freezes and positioning of shots. Work as a team to improve these key areas.

In schedule games, let the skip call the game and give everyone a chance to throw skip and third rocks. You need to improve the finesse shooting of all four players, not just the skip's.

Work as a team. Don't change weights on a shot intentionally without letting everyone know. Keep team communication at a high level. Let the third and skip have some freedom to use their feel in making big shots.

Consider this example. The skip is asked by

A good team calls and sweeps right to the end—Paul Gowsell (left) and Doug McFarlane and Kelly Stearne (sweepers).

the front end, "What weight are you playing?" The reply is "bumper weight." However, the shot doesn't work out quite right and the second says, "That wasn't enough weight on said bumper!"

But a skip can't make the quality shots by being forced to play an exact weight like bumper. Rather, he looks at the shot, sees the amount of ice, reviews the path of the stone, considers sweeping and considers the manner in which his release has been causing rocks to curl. All this adds to a certain feel for the shot.

Allow this "feel for the shot" to flow a little freely for the third and especially for the skip, who has been reading the ice the most and must play most precisely on the team. Let experience flow into the shot; let feel flow into the shot. In the example just described, it would have been better for the skip, when asked about weight, to reply "bumper to down," meaning bumper weight but perhaps a little less, as the shot requires "feel" in that range.

Understanding Pebble

To understand curling ice ask yourself the following questions: What techniques did the caretaker use to make the ice (some plane it centre high or centre low)? What technique is used for pebbling the ice (some pebble once down the centre, some pebble each side)? What is the condition of the curling stones (refer to the section on rocks)?

The diagram below shows a sheet of ice. A is pebbled once down the middle. B is pebbled once on each side with a centre overlap. B pebble will tend to develop a high centre.

Most teams now, in the early ends, use the ice with shots such as C and D directed towards the edge of the four-foot and meant to curl to the centre line. The pebble wears two trails (C and D). After one end, the extreme sides are still heavy and often the centre line is heavier than two feet off it—either to C or D. As a result of this type of play, the ice begins to peak after several pebbles and games.

A certain curling rink you know may take a different slope. Use a keen eye to notice these little characteristics.

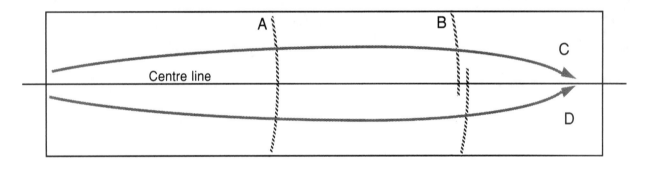

M.B.

Rocks

Why hadn't anyone thought of it before? It seemed so simple. I felt like Thomas Edison.

In the provincial finals in 1983 we had narrowly won a game and one of the rocks that I had played with was 15 heavier for draw weight and almost cost us the game. I lay awake that night thinking and all of a sudden—Eureka! Test out the rocks, I realized.

The next day I tested the rocks as shown in the diagram at the right:

Slide rocks A and B together a distance of 15 feet

The result? Rock B ran away from A by a distance of 12 inches, making A the slower rock.

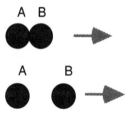

Reverse the order and slide them together a distance of 15 feet.

A did not run away from B because A was the slower rock.

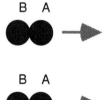

If B is 12 inches faster than A over a distance of 15 feet, then over 120 feet down the ice, the difference could be as much as 10 feet— definitely enough to ruin a shot.

Then I took A and B and tested them against the rest of the rocks my team was throwing. It turned out that A was the culprit. It was 10 to 12 feet heavier down the entire sheet than the rest of the rocks and it curled more as well. It had a slightly different cup or riding surface with a small pit. That day we exchanged it before the game with a stone from another sheet. Thus, luckily Brent, our lead, didn't get stuck throwing it.

That year we won the province and at the Brier we tested all eight of our stones before the game. All the other teams were mystified. What are those guys doing? With an explanation by us, numerous other teams started trying it as well. But they weren't too successful.

There are some rules to follow. The running surface of the two tested stones must be perfectly clean. On setting the rocks into motion, give equal impetus. The two stones are pushed in motion as one (frozen against each other). Both stone A and B have to travel through the same pebble. Thus, select a spot right down the middle of the sheet and have the rocks run true, one behind the other.

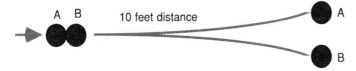

A B   10 feet distance   A

                                            B

The diagram shows an improper trail as the rocks took different paths and encountered varying pebble. As long as the path is true, a trail distance of 5 to 10 feet may be satisfactory for a difference of two to three inches. Then retest to be sure.

It was dumbfounding that I had not thought of the idea earlier in my career. Looking back, many games were affected by not understanding the granite and many were won because the opponent had similar problems.

By the next provincial playdowns and the Brier in Victoria, 1984, everyone was testing the granite, some properly, and many improperly. I had created a monster.

However, while Thomas Edison had turned on the light, only one bulb lit up. Victoria had an arena with lights directed straight downwards and strongly focussed; these together with the television lights created another problem, one that our experience slipped right through.

The method of testing the rocks before the game did ensure, most often, that our particular pair of stones was well matched. But during the odd game in the round robin it seemed players on many different sheets came up with bizarre low percentages while most others were high.

What was happening never struck home until the semifinal. We were playing "the Wrench" (Ed Werenich) and it was hot in the building. In the eighth end our second, Neil Houston, went to peel a guard and raised theirs to the button, with draw weight for two buried behind guards. Then in the ninth end he hogged two and I hogged one. The ice was extremely keen, 13 seconds for draw timed for hog to hog. By the time the tenth end was flashing by me I had realized the problem, but too late.

It goes back to the old natural-ice curling clubs, where in spring, it was warm in the buildings. The ice would be just barely frozen and the rock that was placed upon the backboards for the night would overheat during the day. By the 7:00 p.m. draw they would be 30 feet heavier than in cooler weather. These stones, after stopping and sitting in a certain spot on the ice, would leave a ring impression in the ice after removal. They were sinking into the ice, just as our semifinal Brier game sank.

The viewing of the tapes of the game proved that my theory was correct. Neil's draw weight raise (an attempted peel) was nine seconds hog to hog, while draws were running 13 seconds. In the last 25 feet the rock was melting into the pipes.

We were shooting red handles, the opponents yellow. The reds absorb more heat and some granite is denser and holds more water. Several rocks were sweating, with water pebbles sitting on the large red plastic handles. These water beads acted like little magnifying glasses, thereby increasing the heat to the rock.

The solution would have been so simple. We could have placed white towels over the rocks for a couple of hours before the game to keep the lights off and absorb any water sitting on the handles or granite.

A much overlooked facet of the game is the type of stone used. It's helpful to know the age of the granite, as that will indicate how many years of use the stones have had.

Curling stones are turned over approximately every five years to use the opposite running surface. Of course, you are interested in the present running surface: how many years has it been used? When was the last time it was sharpened?

Rocks that are 20 years old (10 years to a side) will be keen, glide right straight in falls, require less sweeping, roll further, pick up less debris, slide further with strong sweeping and tend to finish differently than new rocks. They are known as dull rocks, as compared to the other extreme—new sharp rocks. New rocks from the factory have a thinner, sharper running surface, one that scrapes more sharply into the ice and creates more friction and grab.

Old rock (upside down) showing thick, flat, dull running surface.

Old dull running cup
- the path it will take

Very little friction on release

Due to low friction, heavy sweeping will straighten rock. Do not oversweep. Let draws go on their own to create a curl.

Will not finish or curl as much in last 30 feet.

Rock can be swept further

May bury or curl well in last 2-3 feet if kept alive by hard sweeping.

Takeouts roll easily

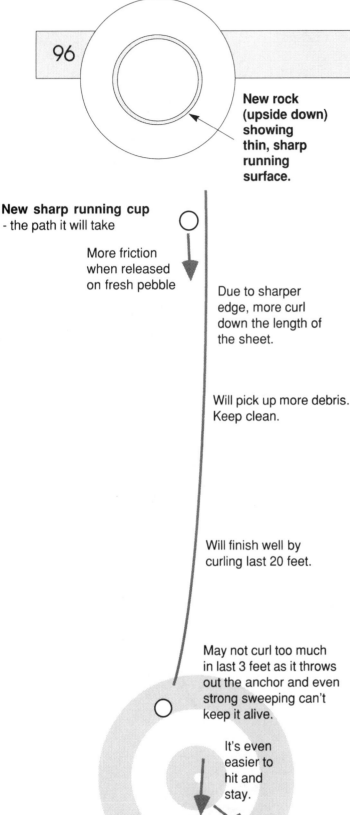

New rock (upside down) showing thin, sharp running surface.

New sharp running cup
- the path it will take

More friction when released on fresh pebble

Due to sharper edge, more curl down the length of the sheet.

Will pick up more debris. Keep clean.

Will finish well by curling last 20 feet.

May not curl too much in last 3 feet as it throws out the anchor and even strong sweeping can't keep it alive.

It's even easier to hit and stay.

This may seem like fine advice but it is not gospel. Sometimes brand-new rocks will run straight until moderately broken in, and different granite thrown into different ice conditions and pebble may work differently as well. However, it's a step in the right direction to have some understanding of the granite. There is a reason for what is going on out there!

Sharpened rocks have different characteristics entirely. Often they are pitted and it takes time for the pits to wear smooth and not affect the running of the stone.

A pitted rock sometimes does the snake dance down the sheet. As the handle rotates, so does the pit. It grabs (curls) the rocks when on one side and releases (straightens) it when it rotates to

A pit is a chip of granite out of the cup. You can feel it by running your fingers over the running cup when you turn the stone over to clean it. Often, early in a game, you will see snow as the pit scrapes more frost off the pebble.

underside of curling stone

pit (hole)

The rock's snake dance

Top view of rock (imagine you can see through to the running surface)

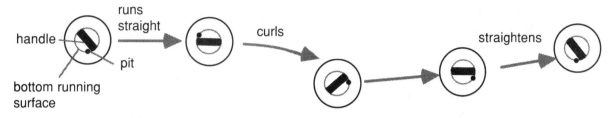

the other side. Place three or four rotations on the stone and watch it dance the snake dance—fun to call the sweep.

It's gone, no, it's falling. It's gone… no, it's falling. The key is to understand where the pit is and as the rock goes down the ice, watch the handle rotation (every half-turn you will get the opposite amount of curl). The pitted stone eventually curls like a normal stone but it gets there in a more entertaining way (it falls, it curls, it falls, it curls).

When you are cleaning the rock off, run your finger along the fine running edge on the bottom of the rock, feeling for little holes called pits.

How Is a Curling Rock Made?*

BY WILLIE KEMP

The story of curling stones is largely a story about people.

It all started 123 years ago when Andrew Kay discovered, judging by demand, that his curling stones were the best in Scotland.

A stone mason by trade, he turned his hand to fashioning curling stones. He created a classic design in his tiny factory on the River Ayr, in Mauchline, Ayrshire, and in those early days all the power came from a water wheel.

Granite is an unwilling partner. Even in the clutches of powerful machines granite kicks back, red-hot sparks fly at the operators and the noise is deafening. Dust and grit are everywhere. A stark contrast to the gentle draw shot which so obediently hides behind a guard with grace and poise.

"It's a labour of love," says James Wylie, the 34-year-old boss of the historic Mauchline factory. He is the third generation of Wylie to be in charge.

"It's a constant battle against all sorts of problems but for our family it has been a way of life."

James Wylie is constantly monitoring the source of supply of basic stone—granite. Stones were not always made exclusively of granite as they are today but one major source, from the quarries on Ailsa Craig, has been terminated.

"Ailsa granite has many of the qualities which we need for top-grade curling stones," says Wylie. "But, to be realistic, the quarrying of the stone on that tiny island [in the Firth of Clyde off Arran Isle] was a hard task and eventually became economically unfeasible.

"Even on a good day at the Ailsa Craig quarry it was a barren place to work. Few would wish to put convicts out there. Mind you, Ailsa Craig granite can still be had. But there was another disadvantage. The Ailsa granite changed colours, at different layers. And when ice rinks demanded their stones should be matched it put Ailsa at a disadvantage."

Over the years, the Mauchline factory has been using Welsh Blue Trevor granite, a steel blue stone with consistent hardness providing longevity of wear. Wylie is currently searching the world for back-up sources of granite, just as a precautionary measure for the future.

Many employees have been with the Kay Co., for years. For instance, Andrew Howie, who specializes in grinding, is a 24-year man. He represents the third important stage of curling stone manufacture.

From square blocks supplied by the quarry, Willie Manson hashes very rough shapes by hand and drills holes down the middle. Fred Nainby, a nine-year worker at Mauchline, then handles the turning of the stones—hard, demanding, tiring work during which granite rebels against fire-hardened steel tools and discs.

Nainby handles five to six stones per day. When he's finished with one it has assumed the recognizable shape of a curling stone and is within one or two pounds of the 40-pound finished article.

Enter Howie, who grinds the remainder while the sparks fly.

Willie Reid, the polisher, represents the way-stop on the production line. His tools combine carborundum stone, sandstone (Ballochmyle), River Ayr home stone and bags of sandstone extracted from earlier stages of development.

Reid needs the patience of a saint for a job that incorporates one of the most vital stages of manufacture, the creation of the running surface. It is the establishment of the running edge which determines the stone's longevity prior to being returned for reconditioning.

A sharp edge will provide a life expectancy, utilizing both sides, of a minimum 10 to 15 years. However, a sharp running edge of 5-inch diameter will run slowly in its early stages of use. Keener stones have less sharp edges, last less long and require factory attention within six years.

Granite with soft flaking properties is of no use for curling stones because consistent hardness is required for a proper running edge. So it is with great love and care that Willie Reid creates the running edge, then polishes out scratches and eventually produces a stone that glistens like a sheer work of art.

At this point, the product is so hot, it is just bearable to touch. Water is used as a cooling agent while the stone is spun at great speed by machine.

Engineer Wylie has developed many special machines now in use for creating the striking band of the stone. In addition to being roughened, the band must have an outward curvature enabling curlers to play some of their favourite chap-and-lie shots.

A diamond cutter applies a fine finishing edge to the top and bottom of the striking band. And with that, the stone is ready for crating and dispatch to wholesale outlets the curling world over.

Restoration after many years of wear and tear constitutes a fair portion of the current workload at the Kay factory. The reconditioning of old Scottish outdoor stones has become popular, likely as a result of the highly successful Grand Match on the Lake of Monteith a few winters ago. Outdoor enthusiasts want to be ready to move at a moment's notice and with the best of equipment.

The Andrew Kay firm is moving to diversity with the manufacture of 25-pound stones for junior curlers and miniature stones for use as gifts, trophies or prizes. Some of the miniatures are made of Italian marble or Skye marble, attractive stone which is not dissimilar to granite but is easier to work.

"Players started right here," he says, "with whin stone. They they realized a better delivery could be achieved if holes for the fingers were carved in the boulders. Use of handles came later, and the landlords always wondered why they were being constantly beaten by the masons who paid more attention to the best stones and the best shapes."

One black stone of particular note in the game's old days was called Crawford John. Still later, the Scots discovered the hard, even granite of Ailsa Craig.

"The Dutch artillery used to substitute the hubs of gun wheels for stones and play a type of curling on the frozen canals," says Wylie.

We've run out of gun carriages today. But Andrew Kay and Company plans to carry on with its vital heritage. The game of curling depends on it.

*Reprinted by permission of the Ottawa Silent Athletic Club, Inc.

Eugene Hritzuk, Saskatoon.

M.B.

Stopwatch

The first person I saw using a stopwatch to time rocks' passage down a sheet of ice was George Fink of the famous Ron Northcott team. For some years many good players shunned the idea of the stopwatch as a means of finding draw weight. However, today a number of top-notch teams use the timing technique.

In practicality, it makes excellent sense: time the number of seconds a draw takes to go from point A to point B. In a heavier spot the rock will be thrown harder, speed down the ice and stop quickly, all taking fewer seconds. In a keen spot, throw easier and the rock will sail along, using up many more seconds as it glides to a stop. Most "watchers" time "hog to hog" for a stone stopping on the tee. Some time from top of

	Hog to hog	Hog to tee	Release to tee	Top of back-swing to tee
Takeout		7 sec.		
Heavier Ice	11 sec.			
Normal Ice	12 sec.	20 sec.	21 sec.	23 sec.
Keener Ice	12.5 sec.			
Keen Spot	13 sec.			
Very Keen Spot	13.5 sec.			

backswing to tee, while other systems use hog to tee or release to tee. The scale above indicates the normal time relationship between the systems.

The hog to hog method is quite accurate. Hog to tee is also fine, except at the time when stones run into guards, etc. Release to tee can be difficult as many players release at varying points. Top of backswing to tee can be used, but a push delivery can upset the timing.

With the hog to hog method for a draw that stops on the tee, add five feet of weight when going from 12 seconds to 11 seconds. (1 second = 5 feet of weight.)

The watch has advantages:

1. Some people relate better to a number than they do to the feel or to their perception. They know what a 12-second weight is at their own club. Thus, they are able to throw a 12-second at a new club.

2. On a brand-new rink (such as the first game at a new bonspiel) it is often easier to time the weight than to observe it.

3. It is excellent for standardizing weight among players. A player's advice can be easily misinterpreted. He may tell his teammate, for example, that the weight is "way keener." But this isn't specific enough, so the teammate overcompensates and hogs the stone. With the explanation that it's a 13.2 second, the player can better gauge the weight.

4. Timing opposition rocks keeps you more involved in the game and you can learn more than normal from their shots.

5. Timing can identify changing ice conditions more quickly and also you can distinguish between keen and heavy trails in the ice.

6. Timing can confirm your suspicions. "It looks keen," you tell yourself. You check the watch, and sure enough, it has changed from 12 to 13 seconds.

7. A team can time takeouts and other weight shots in practice to see if they are all throwing the same type of weight for a particular shot. This provides more team consistency.

8. If a team is practising on your sheet, you can time their shots to get the weight ahead of time.

9. You can time an adjacent sheet on a first end to pick up weight.

There are also disadvantages:

1. Some players rely too much on the watch and forget to use their perception and feel as the main key to draw weight.

2. Some players time their own shots and teammates' shots too much and neglect other important duties such as sweeping, judging and calling of the shot and ice reading.

3. Players take the risk of inviting trouble if their watch malfunctions or they time improperly.

4. Some players on a team don't like the watch and are thrown off when this method is used.

5. Some skips time too much. They should only time a little bit, leaving the rest to front end players, and instead should concern themselves with making good calls and reading the ice accurately.

6. Stop watches can make it awfully noisy out there—*click, click, click.*

Tips on Timing

1. The watch should be used as an aid, supporting perception and feel.

2. Try to time only your opponent's shots. You are too busy on your own shots to worry about timing.

3. The skip should let the front end time the most and rely on their timing advice. This allows the skip to concentrate on more important matters such as ice reading. It also keeps the skip's mind on perception and feel. When he asks the front end player for timing advice, it is as a guide only. When the front end players are responsible for timing, it keeps them in the game and helps team play.

M.B.

Mastering the Release

" Crank you very much."

1. Throw the rock right through the broom.
   Try to hit the broom in such a fashion that the rock looks or feels like it could go right through the broom and straight for 20 feet or so. That is mental follow-through and helps to discourage the flips and turn-ins that can occur in the release.

imaginary line to the broom - - - - - - - - - - - - - - - broom - - - - - - ➔

Mentally extend the
line through the broom.

2. Put the turn on the stone.

There are two theories about this step: the most common approach is to set (or hold) the handle through the slide and put the handle to the straight point on the release. The diagram shows the position of the handle on the rock at various stages of delivery.

A.W.

The inturn comes to the straight position on this release.

Inturn

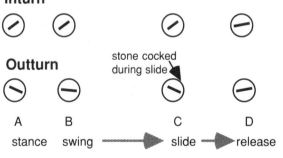

Outturn

stone cocked
during slide

A	B		C	D
stance	swing	$\longrightarrow$	slide $\longrightarrow$	release

The inturn stays cocked slightly throughout delivery and the release goes to the straight point. The turn is put on the stone at the release.

The outturn is set slightly in hack and back-swing and is then cocked a little more during the slide and then released at the end to the straight

M.B.

The outturn is cocked through the slide and then turned to the straight position on the release.

point. Once again the turn is put on the stone at the release.

I often release using this method, but if I'm having a problem it's because I'm putting the turn on the stone too late. So in practice I make the following change. At A and B I keep the position of the handle in stance the same. At C, the beginning of the slide, both turns are cocked appropriately. But now comes the difference. Rather than waiting for the release point to place the turn, I begin to put the turn on right in the middle of the slide. The stone is rotating slightly while in the very light grip of the fingers. The stone actually began the turn that it will have all the way down the ice during the slide. The release becomes simply a follow-through of this action. The diagram below and the three photos that follow illustrate my method.

At the release point, the stone on the inturn has already passed the straight point due to the early turn.

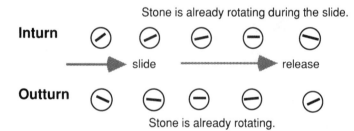

The inturn has already rotated one quarter-turn just after the release because the turn was put on early.

The handle has turned a little more by the time of the release, because the turn began on the stone at an earlier point. This is a smoother release and it eliminates flips and turn-ins. The release becomes a follow-through with the rock still on the fingers. If mastered, this technique is a great way to put on the turn and release the rock. There is far less playing with the stone and the common steering jobs are cut down, too. The method is hard to develop, but it allows a very true release and the rocks can be thrown at the broom more effectively. You will generally need one or two inches more ice for the shot because the handle is put on earlier.

The outturn has already started to rotate early in this slide.

M.B.

3. Use two types of release.

A push release is a special case and that release will be left to those who throw it. Usually pushes require less ice, because the turn is put on late and the rock is given an impetus much like a shot that is set (made to run straight for a long time). Pushers are usually very good drawers and are not quite as good as hitters. They draw well because they bend their arms a little in preparation to push and that gives a better feel of weight than a straight stiff-arm delivery.

The best release is the follow-through release because it continues at the target. Toe sliders' releases are a little different, as their fingers often seem to stay very close to the stone even after release. The flat-foot slider and heel-raised slider should finish with much of the palm facing upwards (more shows upwards on the inturn and half on the outturn). But all that advice goes out the window when you see the fine specialty outturn release of Pat Ryan. His palm looks straight down into the ice on the release as his hand goes over the top of the stone.

A.W.

The palm of the hand faces upwards on the release.

Pat Ryan has his own style. He goes over the top of the rock as the stone's turn is far past the straight point on an outturn.

M.B.

There is another special release that very few curlers use—the jump-off release. Rather than the hand easily following the rock, the hand jumps back from the rock as if it were a hot potato. There is no chance to play with the rock on the release. It is a fast, precise technique. Paul Gowsell used it to perfection. This is an excellent release to practise if you are turning or flipping the normal release. Use it for a while and then gradually go back to your normal style. It might cure it.

A.W.

Once the stone is on excellent line, let the hand jump away as if the stone were a hot potato.

M.B.

"Every time I miss, the skip makes me do push-ups."

Forgetting Your Delivery

Throughout this book you will see references to "forgetting the delivery" and leaving it on the practice ice. There are special little secrets to doing this.

In practice spend the last few shots pretending to concentrate fully on each one and telling yourself that you do not have a delivery. Totally forget that it exists.

In the pregame warmup of mental preparation use two or three sayings (usually centering on building confidence or remembering playing tips) to occupy your mind throughout the match and distract you from any thought of the delivery.

After you throw the stone, don't accept any advice about your delivery technique, even if you miss. Tell everyone that your throw was great and you are going to throw it exactly the same way again. It's easier to adjust the broom at the other end. Nobody in the world hits the broom all the time. Just be consistent. Tell them that next week you'll be missing the broom on the opposite side (wide instead of narrow). Curling often goes just that way.

Concentrate hard on the other fine points of the game when you are in a match—worrying about the delivery is kid's stuff.

M.B.

"Oops, forgot my delivery!"—Don Aitken (nine times Brier competitor).

Section 5
Reaching the Top

Dawn Knowles and Lindsay Sparkes leave
nothing to chance.

Planning Your Year

Plan your curling strategy around two central themes; success and enjoyment. If you are shooting for the top, you may feel that success says it all and enjoyment is secondary. Well, it isn't quite so. Top-notch performances are not built on the backs of aggravation or boredom, but rather on enthusiasm and a love of the sport.

Work hard at improving your game, but have fun at it. Here is a prime example of the wrong way to approach curling. The team plays the same positions all year regardless of the game's importance. The front end is totally bored. They want some of the action in the tighter situations, but they are stuck where they are. After a while the skip has to throw a rock and drag a body. Losing is just over the next hill. The year has been poorly planned. Players have lost the love of the game.

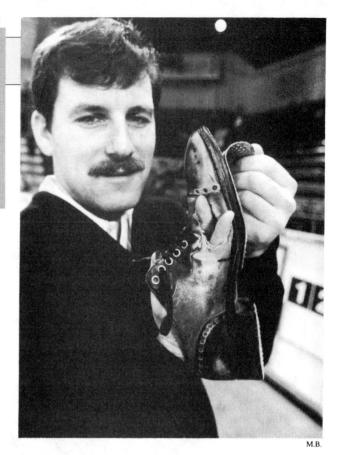

M.B.

You can take an organized approach to the sport without eliminating any enjoyment. At the season's opening, plan out your year, scheduling practices and team meetings and considering events like bonspiels and league games. Set your goals carefully.

The most important decision that you will make all season is your choice of team players. Base the selection on "team unity." For some finer pointers on choosing a winning team, see the section on teams on p.19.

Equipment

Check the condition of your equipment well in advance of the next season. Pay close attention to your shoes, most importantly the slider. It can be disastrous if a sliding shoe rips off during competition and you are forced into a new shoe, with a new slider and a big adjustment on your part. Break a new slider in during practices, long before it is used in a game. Find a slider that is the right speed for your delivery.

In your choice of brooms, whether straw or brush, choose a broom that sweeps well and is clean. Specifically, shampoo your brush and use a fork to clean it out. This removes loose hairs and softens up the bristles so they won't break off.

Slacks and sweater (jacket) should be warm, yet stretchy to allow plenty of flexibility. A vest is a must for the skip to stay warm.

Gloves need to be strong and resilient for sweeping but thin enough to offer good feel in throwing. Skips often wear mitts over gloves to keep their hands warm.

Very important: if you wear glasses, see your optometrist well before the start of the season.

Don't let your boots kick the heck out of your game!

The score-board in curling is an excellent eye test. You will want to able to see the numbers accurately from the far end of the rink.

Entering Bonspiels

A bonspiel schedule has to be packed into the months of October, November and December if you want to total 100 to 150 games for the year. Teams will often experience machine-like play around the 80-100 game levels. As circumstances dictate (money, free time, etc.), each team's input will vary. However, in today's tough bonspiels (especially the pro circuit) it's not smart to play without the regular four. Adding a new player to the lineup for one weekend just doesn't work often enough. The winning teams are playing together at all the spiels and it is tight teamwork that is paying off.

For up-and-coming players, it's a great idea to curl with as many people as possible. You always learn something from everyone. Also, play as many spiels as you can, in and out of town, to gain experience.

When selecting bonspiels sign up for the favourites or *must* spiels, but try not to play too many in a row. Play two or three weekends and then take a break. Bonspiel burnout can easily occur.

Every season try to stretch to the top of your game. There is no sense in playing only where you know you can win—you must travel and play the toughest opposition available. You have to learn to play the best and to be tops you have to beat the best.

Organizational Meetings

This is primarily a forum to make those off-ice decisions and to assign individual duties for the season. All four players should be involved in some way. Simply showing up for practices and games isn't enough. Each player must provide a push.

In the first team meeting, list the tasks of entering bonspiels and leagues, booking hotels,

An outer space bonspiel van.

and flights, reserving practice ice, calling everyone about practice, finding outfits, lining up sponsors and arranging practice games. Split these duties up among the team players. Make sure everyone contributes an off-ice effort.

Setting Goals

Is it necessary to state your goals in the team forum? "Let's win the world championship and five bonspiels as well." For some teams that kind of statement is just the right catalyst. For others, setting interim goals is important, such as: "Let's try to qualify in the first three bonspiels." Some top-notch teams never speak of their dream goals. They are intuitively understood because of the close relationship of the players.

Curling is a pressure game and some teams, as a way to avoid pressure, play extremely hard but avoid the must-win philosophy. Rather, they let it happen. They recognize their talent and feel comfortable with themselves and their playing. Such teams thrive on competition, but avoid setting ultimate goals. These goals, nevertheless, are always in the back of their minds.

However, up-and-coming teams need to concentrate on goals and challenges openly. Try to set ultimate goals and stage your goals as well. Stage goals are good benchmarks of success.

Leagues to Enter

A team that is playing all the bonspiels together should not play more than one league game a week, as a unit. In that game it is often desirable to change positions. Boredom with a position is a curler's archenemy. It is better yet if the lead, second and third skip their own teams in leagues once a week. This allows them to practise the skip-like shots that are so necessary when playing in strong competition.

Setting Attitudes

Take the time to discuss acceptable sportsmanship for the upcoming season. If one team member is a rock-kicker or broom-cruncher, it upsets the whole team. It particularly damages the skip's confidence. It is preferable for all four players, not just one, to show anger, but always keep intense reactions in check. Best of all is four players who are able to control their emotions, without anger, and instead are prepared to retaliate constructively as a team unit. Set up a team reaction to a missed shot. Stress the need for a team reaction, not an individual reaction. This is a team game. For more information on the important topic of team attitudes, see p.19.

Time Out

A break during the season is welcome and healthy. Play plenty of two-on-two after the break to bring everyone back to normal. The key to getting back in tune after a break is the skip. He must get used to shooting pressure shots once again.

Chernoff's Rule

Mike Chernoff, who curled with me for a number of years, was a person who often liked to theorize about curling. He had a double-edged theory of 75%.

First of all, he maintained that during the curling season, it is very difficult for a team to win more than 75% of their games. He compared it to baseball. In 160 games of baseball during the year, a professional baseball team is very fortunate to win 65% of their games. In hockey, 65% or 70% is a good winning record. And in many of these sports, anything over 50% is considered a good record.

In curling, his theory reasoned, it is sometimes possible to play higher than that because there are scheduled games that allow you to play against easier teams. But over a season of perhaps 150 games, the majority of games are played against very tough teams.

Now, I would always argue with him that we could play during the year and aim at winning 90% of our games. He used to laugh at me. "Ah, if you play well," he would say, "you can easily

M.B.

Mike Chernoff in action.

win 50% of your games. If you play a little bit better you can win that extra 25%. But the last 25% you probably can't do anything about. The other fellow will simply curl better than you, or luck will be the factor, or you simply won't have your best day."

We would perhaps be nine out of ten early in the year, or 19 out of 20 from the start of the year, but by the time we neared 100 games, we were having an exceptionally good season if we were there with 75 wins. And if we were 78 or 80, or 85 wins out of 100, that was truly extraordinary. Most often, by the time we reached that game level of 120 or 140, we were very fortunate if we were at 75%.

I think the theory is quite an accurate one now that I have played for a number of years. You simply can't do anything about 25% of those games. You are against a red-hot team or you are a little flat yourself, or luck just doesn't go your way. So a big part of curling is learning how to lose. Even though you are going to play as well as you possibly can, you are still going to lose probably 25% of your games or more; and at times, in bad streaks, you will win 50% or less. So you have to learn how to lose and be able to rebound. At times you can get hot, winning 10 in a row or 11 out of 12.

The second stage to Mike's theory of 75% is a rather rough one. He believed that you have to curl with a 75% success rate or you won't be successful. That is particularly true for almost every event you play. Take a look at the 1985 and 1986 world curling championships—Hackner is in 1985, I am in 1986. Both teams were six and three after the round robin, both times having to win the last two games to go to eight and three, which is a percentage of 73% wins, approximately. If we had lost the final game alone, then we would have dropped to a percentage of 64%, well below the 75% average.

In every bonspiel you enter, if there are 32 teams and eight qualifiers in a cash spiel you are qualifying 25% of the teams. Thus, you have to be better than 75% to qualify. And quite often if you are down in the C event, your final game to qualify you for the eight teams is a game that will see you either fall below 75% or move above it. That percentage stands out as a key point to which you must play.

As a matter of fact, the theory of 75% can actually win you the Alberta Provincial Brier Playdowns. At all levels through the City, the Southerns and the Provincials it is a triple knock-out. You will find, by the number of games played at each level—first of all in Calgary and in the Southerns—that if you qualify for the next level you automatically will have won 75% or better. If you do not qualify you will find that you won below the 75% level.

In the Provincials, your last test to go to the Brier, if you go undefeated in the triple knockout —great. If you have only one loss you are certainly well above 75%. But if your record at the end is seven and two, that will give you a win and a percentage of approximately 78%. If you lost that final game and went to a record of six and three instead, your percentage then would be 66% and you would be a loser.

In the long run you will find in curling that at all levels, it is the team that can maintain this 75% average that will be around at the end for the finals. Now this theory does not hold water for sudden death games. You can be 11 and 0 in the Brier final and lose the final game and be out. You can be 10 and 0 in the final of the Silver Broom and lose the finals, as Scotland did in 1986 when it ended up in second place. The theory of 75% does not apply when it comes to sudden death games, but it's a highly reliable indicator for all the others. So, win 75% of your regular games and always win your final game.

Men's Cash Bonspiels

Here is a listing of recent national bonspiels and
their cash prizes.

Place and Date	Event	Location	Total	1st Prize
Montreal (Sept. 25-28)	Golden Chieftain	Glenmore Curling Club	$25,000	$5,000
Toronto (Oct. 16-20)	Labatt's Eager Beaver	Annandale Curling Club	$12,000	$4,000
Winnipeg (Oct. 10-14)	PWA Classic	Granite Curling Club	$42,000	$12,000
Calgary (Oct. 11-14)	Diamond Jubilee Kick-off	North Hill Curling Club	$12,000	$4,400
Kelowna (Oct. 17-20)	PWA Carspiel	Kelowna Curling Club	$44,000	$28,000
Ottawa (Oct. 20-27)	Molson Masters	Ottawa Curling Club	$15,000	$6,000
Longlac (Oct. 16-20)	5th Annual Labatt's Super Bowl of Curling	Longlac Curling Club	$35,000	$12,000
Saskatoon (Oct. 18-20)	Molson's Pot of Gold	Nutana Curling Club	$15,700	$5,000
*Kitchener (Oct. 25-27)	Glayva Carspiel	K-W Granite	$11,500	$5,000
Vernon (Oct. 24-27)	Vernon Carling O'Keefe Carspiel	Vernon Curling Club	$45,000	$28,000
Toronto (Oct. 29-Nov. 9)	Classic	Royal Canadian Curling Club	$44,000	$12,000
Thunder Bay (Nov. 1-3)	Sun Life Grand Prix	Port Arthur Curling Club	$32,000	$10,000
Kamloops (Nov. 1-4)	Labatt's Crown of Curling	Kamloops Curling Club	$38,000	$12,000
Prince Albert (Nov. 9-11)	Lobstick Spiel	PA Golf and Curling Club	$15,400	$3,400
Kenora (Nov. 15-17)	Lake of the Woods Cashspiel	Kenora Curling Club	$16,000	$5,400
Calgary (Nov. 8-11)	Wardair Classic	Calgary Curling Club	$63,000	$22,000
Fort Francis (Nov. 14-17)	Red Dog Inn Grand Sweep	Fort Francis Curling Club	$15,500	$5,000
Regina (Nov. 14-17)	Molson Open	Regina Curling Club	$36,000	$14,000
Portage la Prairie (Nov. 22-25)	Portage Cash	Portage la Prairie Curling Club	$15,000	$5,000
Dryden (Nov. 22-24)	Big Max	Dryden Golf and Curling Club	$21,700	$5,000
Sarnia (Nov. 22-24)	Sarnia 3rd Annual Cashspiel	Sarnia Golf and Curling Club	$14,600	$6,000
Brampton (Nov. 15-18)	Bacardi Rum Cashspiel	Brampton Curling Club	$9,400	$4,000
Nipawin (Nov. 21-24)	Nipawin Royal Labatt's Auto Classic	Nipawin Evergreen Centre	$51,000	$29,000
Abbotsford (Nov. 29-Dec. 2)	Labatt's Curling Classic	Abbotsford Curling Club	$37,500	$10,000
Whitby (Nov. 28-Dec. 1)	Sun Life Invitational	Whitby Curling Club	$22,000	$7,000
Saskatoon (Dec. 11-14)	Bessborough-PWA Curling Classic	Nutana Curling Club	$50,000	$18,000
Edmonton (Dec. 5-9)	Poor Boy Bonspiel	Shamrock Curling Club	$12,000	$5,000
Swift Current (Dec. 13-15)	Molson Spiel of Fortune	Swift Current Curling Club	$10,000	$4,000
Dartmouth (Dec. 6-8)	Budget Curling Classic	Dartmouth Curling Club	$17,000	$5,000
* Guelph (Dec. 27-29)	Schenley Cashspiel	Guelph Curling Club	$10,000	$3,000
		GRAND TOTAL	$787,800	$294,200

*If same team wins both spiels, an additional $25,000 will be awarded to the winning team.

"My favourite bonspiel!"

Europe
Berne, Switzerland (Oct. 24, 25, 26) Bund
   Trophy 6,000 Swiss francs
Ayr, Scotland (Oct. 31, Nov. 12) Ayr Challenge
   $5,000 (Canadian)
Edinburgh, Scotland (Nov. 28, 29, 30)
   Edinburgh International £2,650

Ladies' Bonspiels

Place and Date	Event	Total	1st Prize
Calgary (early October)	Labatt's Autumn Gold Classic	$20,000	$6,500
Kelowna (mid-October)	Pacific Western Men's/Ladies' Carspiel	over $36,000	Four new cars
Kamloops (late October)	Kamloops Ladies' Curling Classic	$20,000	$6,000
Toronto (late October, early November)	Royals Classic	$23,000	$3,000
Saskatoon (mid-November)	Mid-Winter Classic	$23,000	$7,500
Lethbridge (late November)	Pot of Gold	$4,000	$1,000
Cranbrook (early April)	Cranbrook Tournament of Champions		$1,000

"Fast Eddie" in 1978.

Provincial Playdowns

Winning your province to go to a national championship is a tremendous honour and feat. Many great curlers never make it, even though they are excellent in cash bonspiels. Some try for as long as 20 or 25 years. It's as big a thrill to win out in your province as it is to win a national title. Only once a year do you get that chance. If you don't make it, people will comfort you by pointing out that you will have another chance next year. But it can seem like an eternity till the next chance.

There's always another bonspiel in a week, but there's only one chance to win a "heart" per year.

The pressure in a provincial playoff can be just as great or even greater than in the nationals. Many teams in a provincial final may have been trying for five to ten years to make this step to a Brier or a Scotts Tournament of Hearts and the pressure has really built up.

Ask any player who has been in several nationals and you will hear the same reply: Winning that heart never becomes less of a thrill.

M.B.

"Where did you get the pretty purple coasters?" Fred
Storey has seven but Garnet Campbell needn't feel bad.
He has ten.

National Events

The Brier

The Brier is the showcase of Canadian men's
curling events. More than 80,000 curlers across
Canada start out annually. Only 48 end up representing the 10 provinces, plus Northern
Ontario and the Territories, in pursuit of the
Labatt Tankard, which is made of gold and is
worth more than $50,000.

The Brier has been staged in every province
and 16 different Canadian cities, including every
capital city. When you march on the ice for the
opening ceremonies and the bagpipes begin to
play, it's the sweetest sound in the world.

There are a number of differences between a
Brier and the normal bonspiel. Be prepared for
the contrasts. Here are a few hints that will help
you to keep your feet on the ground.

1. Be prepared to run around like mad in the
week before you leave; even if you try to get
everything done well in advance, it seems that
outfits, tickets, multi-pins to trade, practice,
press, all seem to be last-minute chores. But the
stress does create excitement and a feeling of
urgency.

2. Upon arrival you'll meet your drivers and
other committee members. These are fabulous
volunteers. They have devoted perhaps a year to
meetings and setting up. Often there are 500-

M.B.

The sweetest sound in the world—the bagpipes at the Brier.

1,000 people on a Brier volunteer committee. They really make the event for the curlers.

3. There are people from all across Canada and other countries as well who have attended every Brier for anywhere from five years to 20. It's an annual ritual for them. They love it and are tremendous fans.

4. You'll be expected to attend rules meetings, press conferences, suppers, dinners, breakfasts. Prepare to go the distance. You'll need staying power.

5. The sponsor, Labatt's Brewery, will treat you well and many of their excellent reps from across Canada will be there.

6. As TSN, the television sports network, covers two games per day, be ready for a game of yours to be telecast live. Your skip will be asked to wear a microphone. CBC will request the same coverage for semifinal and final.

7. If you're intending to be one of the three teams left in the playoffs, keep track of one set of rocks of red and one set of yellow to use in these games. You can take these from any sheet and they needn't be a set of eight for the whole team. For example, the lead takes two reds off sheet A, second two off sheet D, etc. Select both red and yellow as you could be playing with either colour in the semifinals and the finals.

8. Don't let the fact that you are representing your province get to you. You're still playing for yourself at this stage too.

9. The spouses are a great asset and can really enjoy themselves.

10. For the 1987 Brier at Edmonton, ladies' seating plans were finally set right. Previously the wives or girlfriends would always get four seats behind one sheet, perhaps sheet A. That was fine when their team curled on sheet A, but once the teams changed sheets for every draw, seeing the game became a battle. In Edmonton a computer system was set up whereby the players' partners received a book of tickets at the outset, moving them behind the proper sheet with every changing draw. The scheme was absolute genius.

11. Practice sessions on the sheet to be played are allowed for both teams prior to the game. The team that practises last has the advantage of realizing just how much the pebble has worn off. Be prepared to time their draws if you practised first.

12. If you're doing well, perhaps leading the pack, prepare to get killed by some team on Thursday evening. It's always been the fateful night at the Brier. Most teams that have won Briers have been drilled on Thursday evening. It's a night of pressure build-up and the bubble wants to burst. Don't be too amazed when it happens. You are not the first.

13. Percentage sheets for shot-making are kept for each game and they are available before the next draw. They are excellent indicators of whether the ice is generally playing better for hits or draws and they can tell you a fair amount about your next opponent.

14. The Brier now pays the way for a fifth man, who can act as an excellent spotter for your team and coach. He is allowed to practise with you as well. Keep this extra player prepared for the playoffs in case of injury.

15. There is a raft of officials on ice, at the hogs, in the gondola, ready to parachute in to pull your rock off if you go over the hog. In 1986 over 20 rocks were pulled off. Be prepared to play within the rules: proper position to stand, sweeping techniques, hog line releases, etc.

16. Expect the ice to be good and the rocks matched as well. Both these areas have really improved in the last few years.

17. Be prepared for some very tough competition.

M.B.

Al Hackner and Ed Werenich help Prime Minister Brian Mulroney open the 1986 Brier in Kitchener. Hec Gervais has just drawn the button with the opening stone.

M.B.

The team photo—"Mr. Prime Minister, would you please move a little to the left?"

M.B.

How to Win the Brier
BY ED WERENICH

It is every curler's dream to win a provincial championship and represent your province in the Labatt Brier. I have competed six times in the Brier since 1973 and in 1983 I was the Labatt Brier Champion and the Silver Broom Champion.

When playing in a championship a team has certain obligations to meet and social functions to attend that can be very distracting. Plan your time carefully so that practice time can be used effectively.

It's a good idea to use your spare time sensibly, too. Get your mind off curling. Play video games or play golf to change your concentration pattern so that you can forget about the pressures of the games ahead.

You have to remember to match the rocks that the team member is throwing. I am convinced that this strategy was a major factor in our team's winning of the Labatt Brier in Sudbury in 1983. By matching the rocks carefully we were able to concentrate fully on playing.

Be prepared for the demands you must meet in

M.B.

Brier fans know how to enjoy themselves.

this particular competition. The Brier is played on arena ice and this creates very different playing conditions. The frost can creep in on the edges as the game progresses. The audience is another factor that adds to the pressure. The noise of the crowd cheering or booing a good shot or a bad one can unnerve an already tense team. Timing your delivery of a stone is very difficult in an arena with a vocal audience that reacts to every shot.

Watch the other games that are in progress and try to deliver your shot when there is a lull in the action. The sweepers must be able to hear the directions of the person supervising play in the house, without running the risk of miscommunication.

There is another important point to remember at the championships. Congratulate your teammates on a good shot as often as possible. Everyone feels the pressure of the limelight and a positive word will increase your team's confidence.

As for yourself, control your emotions throughout the championships. Don't get too excited about making a good shot, nor too disappointed about a bad shot or a bad break. You will play your best when you stay alert but relaxed.

M.B.

The hog-line rule is now closely called at national playoffs. John Base officiates at the 1986 Brier.

The Scott Tournament of Hearts
BY MARILYN DARTE

Challenge is a word our team enjoys both on and off the ice. Winning and losing some of those challenges is only half of the experience. The other half is the personal insight and overwhelming emotion of the curling game. We play our game aggressively and with flair because we are enjoying each other and the game itself.

Playing the recent ladies' curling championships, the Scott Tournament of Hearts, in our home province of Ontario was exciting for our team. We used this hometown advantage as fuel for the week of play. Our most exciting games took place in the London Arena. The desire to win was the bottom line for all of us personally and no obstacle would stand in our way. We decided in our team meeting before the Canadian championships to take each rock, each game as it comes. Our team motto was to deal with the situation at hand and just let it happen.

M.B.

Left to right, Chris Jurgenson, Marilyn Darte, Kathy McEdwards and Jan Augustyn.

Linda Moore of B.C., 1985 Ladies' World
Champion.

Teammates need to trust one another and
communicate throughout the game—Marilyn
Darte and teammates, 1986 Ladies' World
Champions.

M.B.

International Events

The Silver Broom

Ten countries play off for the men's world curling championship every year. The two teams that place at the bottom of the heap are now challenged each fall by other countries trying to win their way in. It is hoped that Japan, the newest county to join this competition, will be admitted soon.

In the early years the award was the Scotch Cup. Then for many years the Air Canada Silver Broom was awarded and in 1986, for the first time, the President's Cup trophy was presented.

M.B.

M.B.

The Silver Broom is a cherished victory—Eigel Ramsfjell, Norway, 1984 World Men's Champion.

M.B.

In the early years the award was the Scotch Cup. Then for many years the Air Canada Silver Broom was awarded and in 1986, for the first time, the President's Cup trophy, shown above, was presented.

World Curling

BY RICK LANG

Each year the curling season is highlighted by the three world championships: Men's, Junior Men's and Ladies'. To have the opportunity to compete at these levels is indeed rare. Approximately 80,000 Canadian men enter the playdowns each year and only four individuals succeed.

There is little doubt that Canada is the best curling nation in the world—we have the best facilities, the most players and the highest level of competition. However, due to good coaching (mostly by Canadians) several European countries have produced top-calibre teams.

The men's world championship originated in 1959 as the Scotch Cup, a series of challenge games between Canada and Scotland. The U.S.A. joined the competition in 1961 and since then the championship has grown to 10 competing countries with several others clamouring to be included. The 1986 championship held in Toronto was televised live in Britain and Canada. The event has grown into a highly competitive, dramatic and tension-packed finale to every curling season.

The junior men's world championship developed out of a yearly competition held at the East York Curling Club in Toronto. The bonspiel always included junior teams from Canada as well as Europe. With major sponsorship and national television coverage, this event is now the showcase for the men's champions of the future.

The ladies' world championship, inaugurated in 1979, is the youngest of the three world championships. Four different countries have already won the ladies' world championship and this shows the popular, competitive nature of the event.

Playing in a world championship is the ultimate thrill for any athlete and naturally it produces the greatest amount of pressure. It takes years of dedication and hard work to perfect the talents required to achieve this level and once there, you realize that it is entirely possible that this may be your one chance to win it all. Of all the teams that curl in the world championship each year, only one team ends the year on a victorious note. The difference between finishing first and second is astounding. When you win the Canadian Brier and represent Canada at the world championship, you are representing your entire country—a country that prides itself on being the best curling nation in the world. At the Brier level you represent your province, and your fellow curlers at home expect you to do well. But when you represent Canada, not only your fellow curlers but the entire national population expect you to win. With the ever-increasing public awareness of our game, combined with the pride Canadians have in their athletes, the pressure is tremendous.

The Canadian Brier is held in early March and the world championships are played three to four weeks later. This leaves very little time to make the necessary arrangements and ensure proper mental preparation. Many European countries name their national champions earlier. They are able to do this because they have fewer teams competing. This lead time allows them to prepare properly.

Another difficulty facing the Canadian team is the length of the playdown system. Most Canadian curlers start their playdowns in December and the provincial championships are determined in February, approximately 25-30 games later. Three weeks afterwards, the Brier is held. Gruelling is the only word to describe this event. The winner will have played 12 to 13 games in a seven-day span. Most teams are able to handle the physical requirements but the mental stress can prove unbearable. A Brier victory means another four weeks of anxiety and tension as you get ready for the once-in-a-lifetime opportunity.

Most curlers dream of this opportunity, but the reality of the situation soon sinks in. You and your team have played 40 intense, crucial games over the last three months. You have achieved a great feat in winning one of Canada's great sporting events—the Brier. Now you are representing Canada. If you win the world curling championship you are a hero. If you come in second you are a bum! It's as simple as that.

We cannot tell you how other countries prepare for the championship, but we can give you an idea of how Canadians prepare. It is safe to say that as the winners of the national championship your team is playing well and each player has no serious problems. You must then develop an appropriate game plan, and prepare mentally.

All teams and conditions are different so it is difficult to suggest a strategy that would work for all teams in all cases. There are, however, some constants:

1. Europeans play throughout the year on faster and straighter ice than Canadians do (their

M.B.

Bernie Sparkes instructs eager Japanese curlers.

curling stones are worn!). This results in the Europeans playing a simpler, wide-open game.

2. Canadians play more games under more varied conditions than other countries.

3. Due to these varied conditions, Canadian curlers have more experience in strategy and finesse shot-making.

If Canadians are to play their strength they must play a strong offensive game with many rocks in play. Naturally the wise Europeans keep the game simple and test the patience of the Canadians.

The danger of developing such a game plan is that you can only do what the conditions allow. If the ice is fast and straight, Canadians are forced to beat the Europeans at their own game and that can be a difficult chore.

Proper mental preparation is the real key to winning a world championship. Many great Canadian teams have won the Brier only to lose the World, and they spend their entire summer explaining what happened.

Whether we like it or not, Canadians have underestimated the opposition. The Europeans are good. So are the Americans and very soon, the Japanese and maybe the Russians. Not many would argue the fact that Canada has the best teams, but we must realize that our best is equalled by the best of many other countries.

It was not many years ago that Canadian curlers openly stated that their prime goal was the Brier and that the world championship was anticlimactic. Not only is this dangerous thinking, it is wrong. Canadian teams must not only maintain their Brier intensity—they must increase it. The whole year must build from the club playdowns through the world championships. If you think winning the Brier is the ultimate goal, think again. The other teams at the World will walk all over you and you may spend the rest of your life saying "if only I had that chance again."

Maintaining your intensity comes directly as a result of respecting your opposition. The rest of the world knows how to play, they are well coached and more than anything else, they want to beat Canada! They will play their best game of the round robin against you, so you can never let up. Be ready to give it all you've got.

The world curling championships are great events. There are no pros or amateurs—everyone is eligible. There are no free agents or huge contracts: no one has ever bought a world curling championship. So far, we have avoided any political difficulties. There has never been a boycott, nor any disputes about the refereeing. Yes, indeed, when you win a world curling championship you can claim to be the very best in the world and no one can dispute the results. Very few sports can make the same claim!

To Boot or Not to Boot*
BY BOB PICKEN

For 20 consecutive men's world curling championships, Bob Picken has served as a CBC curling commentator. He started at the Scotch Cup in Perth, Scotland, in 1967. He witnessed the most dramatic moment in world curling history, in 1972.

Saturday, March 25th. It came up sunny and glorious again, with the temperature near 15 degrees. Meleschuk waltzed to an 8-3 victory over Scotland's Alex Torrance in the semifinals. It was Canada's 28th straight Silver Broom win, dating back to American veteran Bud Somerville's triumph over Northcott in the round robin at Perth, Scotland, in 1969. It seemed just a formality to make it 29 in a row that evening against Robert Labonte of the United States.

The 21-year-old Labonte had other ideas. He drew the four-foot with last stone on the first end to score two. Meleschuk blew a takeout on the third end, and the American hit the house for two more to lead 4-1. It went to 5-1 on the fourth when Labonte put a wall around another counter.

Two more ends, an exchange of deuces and

"Boots" Labonte and the "Big O" Meleschuk ham it up years after the fateful kicked rock.

the Americans were still in front 7-3. Only four ends to go, and Canadians suddenly were decrying the switch made at the 1972 Broom to go from 12- to 10-end games to facilitate television.

The Big O went to catch-up curling. His team didn't quit. Two on the 7th, then a break. Labonte was feeling the pressure. He missed both takeouts on the 8th. Meleschuk stole two points, and it was all even 7-7.

The comeback stalled on the 9th. Canadian third Dave Romano fanned on a hit. The North Dakota crew cashed the opportunity, scored a two, and they were in the driver's seat, up 9-7 going home.

The finish of the 10th end was bizarre. The Americans had it tantalizingly close, but they were tighter than a drum. Two misses and Meleschuk had three counters. But Labonte responded and made a superb double takeout with his last stone.

Orest was left with a partial come-around to hit

the U.S. shot stone in the four-foot circle. Canada had second shot, and another American stone was third, about halfway into the eight-foot ring. There were a couple of other biters, but they were inconsequential. Meleschuk had to hit and stick to tie.

He played his inturn with medium weight. It punched out Labonte's counter, but spun to the left and U.S. third Frank Aasand was on it like a hawk. He swept the Canadian stone into the eight-foot, then halfway into the 12-foot where it came to rest. Did Canada count one or two?

In the next few seconds, Aasand thought he was a world champion. He took a quick overhead look at the Canadian stone, then his own, raised his broom in the air and jumped with glee. He did the dance clear of the stones, something his skip didn't do seconds later.

Aasand's action was his alone. Canada's Romano had a chance to study the position of only the American stone. Before Romano could move to check the Canadian stone, Labonte made the boot that rates as the greatest *faux pas* in the history of curling.

Reacting to Aasand's victory dance, Labonte came forward, started to jump, lost his balance and landed on his back—kicking the Canadian stone in the process.

Aasand reached down and pulled Labonte's foot aside. But it was too late. The stone had been moved and Romano saw it. So did several thousand witnesses, and the gasp went through the arena: "HE KICKED IT!"

Canada should have been awarded the two points and the tie immediately. But umpire-in-chief Doug Maxwell was directly behind Labonte and didn't see the kick. He asked Aasand, "Did you kick it?" The American said, "No." Nobody asked Labonte the same question in the midst of the shock and uncertainty.

Maxwell decided the only course was to measure the two stones. Perhaps fortunately, the Canadian stone at least now was a half-inch winner, and the tie was declared.

Labonte could have made amends. He had the

hammer on the extra end. But Meleschuk made one of the most perfect clutch draw shots I've seen in international curling. He buried in the four-foot behind two guards and the party was over. Labonte was heavy, sailed on past, and Canada had a 10-9 victory.

Some called it a tainted title.

Somebody invented the Labonte Curse because Canada failed to win the Silver Broom in the next seven years.

I saw Robert Labonte several times after the fateful day in 1972. He kept trying to get back to the world championship. Two years ago he told me in Duluth, he knew he'd never make it.

Was he bitter? No way. Robert likes to play the guitar and sing his own little ballads. He has one super little ditty, about curling being "Nothing But A Pain In The Butt."

* Reprinted by permission of the Toronto Silver Broom 1986 Inc. organizing committee.

Pioneer World Ladies' Curling
BY MARILYN DARTE

After winning the Scott Tournament of Hearts, our team was faced with a three-week waiting period before the World's began. Because we had received so much press coverage after the Canadian championships, people kept asking us when we would come down from our high. Our feet never left the ground because our main goal was to win the world title for Canada. Everyone expects the Canadian team to win the world championship every single year and the pressure that causes is enormous. But we did not succumb to the pressure. Our experience and confidence carried us through. Each member had a job to accomplish, and communication was our bond.

Our first goal was to have fun. If we couldn't have fun by playing the sport we all love so much, it wasn't worth the time that such a big commitment requires. When we started to have fun we started to relax. Then the biggest strength in any sport set in, the concentration. When we combined fun, relaxation and concentration, we had our winning formula. I firmly believe that curling is 90% mental and 10% mechanical. It is all in attitude and execution.

We knew going into the World's that we were the best team there and all we had to do was *win*. It sounds easy, but outside pressure could have diverted us from our game plan. We were mentally prepared to be the best. Our preparation paid off and we came home with the title of World Champions.

A Spouse Speaks Out
BY JUDY LUKOWICH

"I'm not Judy, I'm Ed's Wife." This was the message on a T-shirt I was given when Ed won the Canadian championship in 1978.

Spouses in curling, and I imagine any sport, have been through it all. They have been written about, photographed, interviewed and blamed for countless mistakes.

The friend who gave me the T-shirt thought that I was losing my identity. I joke about my public role and sometimes introduce myself as Ed's wife, but I do it all in fun.

I joined the ranks of competitive curling many years ago, so I know what every curler wants— to reach the top. If I can't make it (I'm still trying), what could be better than to have my husband or another family member make it instead? I feel as excited about my husband's accomplishment as if I had won it myself. In a way, I am the winner too.

What great events the Brier and world championships are, when you are attending as the spouse of a competitor. I have often described it as like being queen for a week. You are wined and dined, with many banquets, lunches and little gifts. You even have your own driver.

The Hackner team and their wives celebrate winning the 1985 Brier.

Attending big events does take a lot of preparation in a short period of time, usually accompanied by sheer panic. Arranging to get pins, packing, making sure the uniforms are ready, organizing the tickets and seeing to all the other endless details that may have been overlooked make the days before you leave busy and a little crazy.

But once you arrive, the people you meet, the friends you make and the good times you have, along with the experience you gain, make you forget the stress. I am glad to be part of it all and the encounters along the way have been opportunities I have taken advantage of to help myself personally.

Ladies' Challenge
BY MARILYN DARTE

Wave an Olympic Gold Medal in front of Team Canada 1986 and the World Curling Champions and our team reacts as if you were flashing a red cape in front of a raging bull. We are determined to qualify in the Olympic Trials in Calgary and then go on to win that Olympic Gold Medal. Our team will know we have reached the top when we stand on the winners' podium listening to the strains of "O Canada."

Women's curling is as competitive as the male version. The desire and the attitude are equal for both sexes. In the ladies' curling circuit there is

There are ups and downs in the competitive part of the event, but it is a good feeling to be needed and to be supportive. You can expect to be blamed occasionally when things go wrong or too few games are won, but in the height of competition in any sport, tempers flare and emotions can heat up. You have to be mentally prepared, so you can cope with all the moods your mate experiences in the face of competition and pressure. You have to know when to speak up and when to be quiet. Your own patience and peace of mind can be put to the test often in these long weeks.

A.W.

not the same prize money to be won because of lack of sponsorship. This is true for many sports —take golf, for example. Public interest continues to grow, however.

Strategy is the main difference between men's and women's curling games. The majority of women curlers tend to call a weaker game. Men play a more aggressive game. But the strongest Canadian women's teams match the males' aggressive approach. Women shoot just as well as their male counterparts and strength is irrelevant in this sport.

Ladies' curling has come a long way and the women in this sport are still travelling to the top, earning recognition and enthusiasm at every step.

Section 6
Comedy Corner

Brother Mike

Fast Eddie

Doug (Notice the L on his arm. He always wanted to play lead, but we didn't think he was good enough.)

Dave, lead (He was good enough.)

This is one of my favourite curling photos. From top to bottom it's my brother Mike at skip, Doug MacCloud at second, Dave Moore at lead and myself at third. Notice the nice warm sweaters. They're almost back in style. The year was 1961 and we finished second in the Canadian high school championships. The next year, the team stayed together and in 1962 Speers, Saskatchewan had its first ever Canadian champs. I was a foot taller and known as "The Intimidator."

I was born "Fast Eddie" Lukowich, son of Button Joe, in prairieville Speers, a poke and plumb town—"Poke your head out the window and you're plumb out of town."

My pa ran the two-sheeter and at age six they asked me to curl in the school bonspiel because they were short, and I was short too. Well, our skip slipped down onto the back of his head and our third took the helm and led us to victory. It was my first. The prize was a flashlight so I could find my way from Speers east to Speers west. I tried right to the end of high school and never again won that spiel. For millenniums, we flooded that ice in winter and curled our little hearts out. Frost an inch thick, warped ice at 30 degrees below, bumps in spring, and then we would throw it as hard as we could as the ice melted.

I turned down an Oxford scholarship just to stick with my curling game and it's paid off. I now have my very own mortgage!

Drawing Disasters

At the Vernon carspiel, my last rock draw attempt was a wee bit heavy, knocking us out of the spiel. Wes Aman, playing lead, went to the kitchen and asked if my draw had knocked the bacon and eggs off the stove. Then on the way home, Wes looked out the window of the plane and started screaming, "There it is, I've found it, Ed. There's your rock down there by that farmhouse and it looks like it's slowing down." A couple of feet heavy and you can't live it down.

A few years later in Switzerland, in a big game against Jim Ursel, we were one down coming home. The other team was lying two and we had third shot. We could tie the game and go the extra or try the extremely difficult double for the win. The double was nearly straight across; the rock would have to be a howitzer.

I fired and I was a foot wide too. Now, this rock had two chances of curling, slim and none, and slim just left town. The rock crashed the

hack, did a double-wheelie in the air and flopped down.

Later I was sitting in the back of the bus, as nobody wanted to talk to me. All of a sudden I heard this roar of laughter from the front. Someone piped up."Hey Ed, we were wondering. You know that rock you threw tonight and that draw you threw in Vernon, well, they're going to meet in the middle of the Atlantic and there's going to be this huge explosion…" "Aaaah, shut up!"

Gerry Benson was playing third in Medicine Hat and it was my last rock. I wanted to hit their stone sitting close to the boards and roll in. The shot looked close, but I lost sight of it as the sweepers fell in behind and their front end also jumped off the benches. Looking for the roll, all I saw through a mass of legs was Gerry, poised to catch the rock as it bounced off the boards. His hand reached in and picked up their rock and my shooter went right underneath. Gerry had a ghost-like look on his face as he set their stone back down. I took the blame for throwing it too low.

Don Duguid, colour man for CBC, was broadcasting the Silver Broom. A certain European skip idolized him and wanted skipping advice, so he asked Duggy to give him signs from the press box because he was having an awful time with strategy. The signs were: wrong shot, shake your head; right shot, nod your head. He's down 10 and the opposition is laying three. The skip goes over to the shot rock and indicates a freeze, but Duggy shakes his head. Then over to the second shot, but no. Then at the third shot he indicates a freeze, and looks up to Duggy, who nods. Looking bewildered, the skip freezes perfectly to the third shot, leaving the other team a draw for three.

He looks up at Duggy. Duggy shakes his head…

A Horrible Poem

So curling is your game you say
And you think to make it all the way.
Well, practise lots and say your prayers
And hope the errors are all theirs.
'Cause this game has some rounds and rounds
A few good ups but some dastardly downs.

You've a couple up with one to go
Your lead fans two and your second don't show.
So your third steps in as bold as brass
But you'd swear that he'd been smoking grass.
So now it's time for your big draw
But as luck would have it—it grabs a straw.

When your team's as sharp as a butcher's knife
And you can't hit the rings to save your life
Well, it's down to the last and the draw's the play
But you shake your head, "We'll hit and stay."
You let it go as good as gold
But you roll too far and you're down the road.

Do you get mad—oh gracious, no
Mustn't let that Irish temper show.
'Cause we don't care if we win or lose
Either way we still drink the booze.
We smile, shake hands and wish them well
But underneath, it's "Go to hell!"
—Tim (Horrible) Horrigan, Victoria, B.C.

Jim McQuarrie, Lethbridge: "Jim, how'd the game go?"

Jimbo: "Oh, we lost. But we went a couple of extra ends, the fifth and sixth."

Jim sat up in the lounge watching the curling. He pointed out a player to his companion. "See that Bob Thompson out there? He's been playing 15 years and he has three purple hearts on his sweater. I've been playing 20 years and all I have is a yellow liver."

Rick the Mick

Shortly after Al and Rick won the 1982 world curling championship they were flying home to Thunder Bay. Several people were staring at Rick. "Good, they've recognized me!" thought Rick.

The flight attendant approached him and asked, "These people are wondering if you're who they think you are?" He nodded proudly. "Could they have your autograph?" she asked. Then the fans came over and one exclaimed, "Oh Mick, we love your songs!" It turned out that Rick had been mistaken for Mick Jagger of Rolling Stones fame (they do look remarkably alike).

Oh, oh, Rick didn't know quite what to do. As they asked for his autograph, he quickly penned Mick's most illegible signature. Then he started to worry. What if he was mobbed at the airport?

When the plane landed, Rick asked Al to get the luggage while he ran out and grabbed the car. Rick arrived in front of the building as Al raced out with the bags. They made a clean getaway, but it was reported for weeks afterwards that Mick Jagger had been through town. And Rick's nickname now is Rick the Mick, Rock 'n' Roll Lang.

Rick the Mick, Rock 'n' Roll Lang

M.B.

The Gows and Fast Eddie

Paul Gowsell and I were hot as not one of our first six wins went past six ends in the Yellow-knife competition. So there we stood, in the cash, ready to take home first place. Paul commented on the fact that if we could ever get the front end shooting, we would be unbeatable.

Next game, we were leading 3-0 after three ends and what's more, the front end was playing great guns. Going into the fourth, we were shot, although they had three biters at the edge, behind a guard. All we had to do was draw anywhere on the planet to split the rings and force the draw against two.

"The Gows" had perfect weight, but with no sweep and late calling we pulled a mistake of humungous proportions as the stone threw out the anchor. Ouch, good for the umpteenth shot. They made a wide-open hit for four. Pauley and I didn't make another shot and we were totally in the tank. The front end played great. We lost 12-3 in six ends. Well, we never did play more than six ends in the tourney. There is no God.

We had to stay over to catch a charter flight and we decided to drink a few to drown our sorrows. I've been known to pull a few wild antics in my time and the scene was set. I decided

"Help!"

the defeat was the fault of my curling slacks and sweater. They came off and I crammed them into the garbage can and set it on fire. It was getting smoky and stinky, so my teammate Glen fired the can out the door into a snowbank. In the morning we went out for a gander, and there at the bottom of a two-foot hole in the snow lay the charred remnants of a curling year. "That outfit will never lose another game," we declared.

The best eight-ender ever recorded must be the one in Saskatoon. This lady was seven down playing the last end and scored eight to win easily. There's no use playing your best card until it's time. Maybe there is a God.

Getting down with "The Gows."

Section 7
For the Record

Trivia

BY AL HACKNER

We are living in an age of statistics. Every time I read the sports page I am confronted with batting averages, RBIs, yards rushing, touchdown passes, shots on goal and others too numerous to mention. But nowhere do I see a set of curling statistics. It is high time that Canada's most popular sport had its very own set of statistics and I feel duty-bound to provide this service. Here then for your perusal is a set of statistics on one week's play in the ladies' bonspiel:

• there were 21 draws this week.
• if you played in the bonspiel, you curled 10 games.
• you ran 22,617 feet (mostly bent over and backwards), or just over 12 miles.
• you lifted 8,800 pounds of granite, or slightly over 4.4 tons.
• since 8 p.m. Saturday you lifted an average of 172 pounds per hour.
• you threw 200 rocks (some were quite good), that travelled a distance of 25,400 feet.
• in total, 11 skips called "sweep" 718 times and "No, let it go" 715 times. Of these, 694 calls were unnecessary and the balance was helpful to the opposition.

M.B.

Which curler has represented the most provinces at the Brier? Earle Morris (shown above).

Which curler has represented the most provinces in the Canadian Ladies'? Cathy Shaw (Pidzarko)—Manitoba, Alberta, N.W.T.

Multiple Brier Winners—32 names in total

Four-Time Brier Winner	Winning Years
Ernie Richardson, Saskatchewan	1959, '60, '62, '63
Arnold Richardson, Saskatchewan	1959, '60, '62, '63
Garnet Richardson, Saskatchewan	1959, '60, '62, '63

Three-Time Brier Winners	
Howard Wood, Sr., Manitoba	1930, '32, '40
Ken Watson, Manitoba	1936, '42, '49
Grant Watson, Manitoba	1936, '42, '49
Matt Baldwin, Alberta	1954, '57, '58
Wes Richardson, Saskatchewan	1959, '60, '62
Don Duguid, Manitoba	1965, '70, '71
Ron Northcott, Alberta	1966, '68, '69
Bernie Sparkes, Alberta	1966, '68, '69
Fred Storey, Alberta	1966, '68, '69
Bryan Wood, Manitoba	1970, '71, '79
Rick Lang, Northern Ontario	1975, '82, '85

Two-Time Brier Winners	
Gordon Hudson, Manitoba	1928, '29
Ron Singbusch, Manitoba	1928, '29
Bill Grant, Manitoba	1928, '29
Jim Congalton, Manitoba	1930, '32
Ernie Dollard, Manitoba	1931, '40
Cliff Manahan, Alberta	1933, '37
Ab Gowanlock, Manitoba	1938, '53
Bill Walsh, Manitoba	1952, '56
Allan Langlois, Manitoba	1952, '56
Andy McWilliamson, Manitoba	1952, '56
Bill Price, Alberta	1957, '58
Gordon Haynes, Alberta	1957, '58
Hec Gervais, Alberta	1961, '74
Ron Anton, Alberta	1961, '74
Rod Hunter, Manitoba	1970, '71
Jim Pettapiece, Manitoba	1970, '71
Ed Lukowich, Alberta	1978, '86
Al Hackner, Northern Ontario	1982, '85

Multiple Purple Hearts in Briers (six Brier appearances or more)

	Hearts
Bernie Sparks, Alberta/ British Columbia	11
Garnet Campbell, Saskatchewan	10
Don Aitken, Quebec	9
George Dillon, Prince Edward Island	8
Bob Dillon, Prince Edward Island	7
Doug Cameron, Prince Edward Island	7
Fred Storey, Alberta	7
Jim Ursel, Manitoba/Quebec	7
Perry Hall, Ontario	6
Reg Stone, British Columbia	6
Roy Stone, British Columbia	6
Glen Campbell, Saskatchewan	6
Bob Pickering, Saskatchewn	6
Ron Northcott, Alberta	6
David Sullivan, New Brunswick	6
Rick Lang, Northern Ontario	6
Ed Werenich, Ontario	6
Paul Savage, Ontario	6
Howard Stewart, Quebec	6

M.B.

The winner of the most purple hearts: Bernie Sparkes of British Columbia, with 11. Saskatchewan's Garnet Campbell is runner-up with 10.

Most Brier Appearances as:

		Years
Skip (6)	Reg Stone (B.C)	1949, '52, '53, '55, '57, '62
	Jim Ursel (Que.)	1974, '75, '76, '77, '79, '80
Third (6)	George Dillon (P.E.I.)	1958, '60,'61, '63, '70, '77
Second (5)	Sam Richardson (Sask.)	1959, '60, '62, '63, '64
	Don Aitken (Que.)	1970, '72, '75, '76, '77
Lead (7)	Fred Storey (Alta.)	1960, '63, '64, '66, '67, '68, '69

M.B.

Don Aitken from Quebec has nine purple hearts.

Most Brier Games Won

	Appearances	Played	Wins	Losses
Bernie Sparkes, Alberta/British Columbia	11	116	80	36
Garnet Campbell, Saskatchewan	10	101	76	25
Don Aitken, Quebec	9	99	59	40
Fred Storey, Alberta	7	71	56	15
Rick Lang, Northern Ontario	6	73	51	22
Ed Werenich, Ontario	6	71	49	22
Jim Ursel, Manitoba/Quebec	7	76	48	28
Ron Northcott, Alberta	6	61	48	13
Paul Savage, Ontario	6	69	46	23
Glen Campbell, Saskatchewan	6	60	46	14
Ernie, Arnold, Sam Richardson, Saskatchewan	5	52	45	7
Bob Pickering, Saskatchewan	6	61	44	17

Most Losses, One Skip—31
Bud Fisher, Newfoundland, 1957, '58, '59, '61

Most Wins, One Skip—45
Ernie Richardson, Saskatchewan, 1959, '60, '62, '63, '64

Most Appearances
Bernie Sparkes (11), Alberta, British Columbia, 1966, '67, '68, '69, '72, '73, '74, '76, '78, '83, '84

Brier Skips with 25 or More Wins

Skip	Brier Appearances	Briers Won	Games Played	Won	Lost
Ernie Richardson, Saskatchewan	5	4	52	45	7
Reg Stone, British Columbia	6	-	59	41	18
Ron Northcott, Alberta	5	3	51	40	11
Jim Ursel, Quebec	6	1	65	40	25
Matt Baldwin, Alberta	5	3	51	38	13
Al Hackner, Northern Ontario	4	2	51	37	14
Ed Lukowich, Alberta	4	2	47	37	10
Bob Pickering, Saskatchewan	5	-	51	36	15
Cliff Manahan, Alberta	5	2	45	35	10
Hec Gervais, Alberta	4	2	42	34	8
Bernie Sparkes, Alberta/British Columbia	5	-	55	34	8
Gord Campbell, Ontario	5	1	41	30	11
Ed Werenich, Ontario	3	1	40	29	11
Garnet Campbell, Saskatchewan	3	1	30	26	4
Rick Folk, Saskatchewan	3	1	34	26	8
Doug Cameron, Prince Edward Island	5	-	50	26	24
Ken Watson, Manitoba	3	3	27	25	2

M.B.

Don Duguid, twice world champion (1970, 1971), has been the colour man on CBC curling broadcasts for many years.

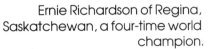

Ernie Richardson of Regina, Saskatchewan, a four-time world champion.

35 or More Hearts per Game in Brier Competition

1971

Saskatchewan	vs.	Newfoundland	or		Manitoba	Total
Pickering	6	Cole	1	Duguid	4	
Campbell	10	Bowering	2	Hunter	2	
Keys	5	Ellis	4	Pettapiece	2	
Ford	4	Andrews	4	Wood	2	
TOTAL	25		11		10	36 & 35

1970

Saskatchewan	vs.	Prince Edward Island	or		New Brunswick	
Pickering	5	Burke	5	Mabey	5	
Campbell	9	Dillon	7	Keith	5	
Keys	4	Sanders	4	Steeves	2	
Ford	3	Burke	1	Bowering	2	
TOTAL	21		17		14	38 & 35

1983

British Columbia	vs.	New Brunswick		
Sparkes	10	Sullivan	5	
Armstrong	3	Sullivan	6	
Cook	3	Palk	4	
Bauer	3	Cormier	2	
TOTAL	19		17	36

1984

British Columbia	vs.	Ontario		
Sparkes	11	Werenich	6	
Armstrong	4	Savage	6	
Thompson	2	Kawaja	2	
Heintz	1	Harrison	3	
TOTAL	18		17	35

M.B.

Andrea Pavani of Italy, who has played 11 times at the World Curling Championship.

Multiple World Winners—19 names in total

Four-Time World Winners	Winning Years
Ernie Richardson, Canada	1959, '60, '62, '63
Arnold Richardson, Canada	1959, '60, '62, '63
Garnet Richardson, Canada	1959, '60, '62, '63

Three-Time World Winners	
Wes Richardson, Canada	1959, '60, '62
Bill Strum, USA	1965, '74, '78
Ron Northcott, Canada	1966, '68, '69
Bernie Sparkes, Canada	1966, '68, '69
Fred Storey, Canada	1966, '68, '69

Two-Time World Winners	
Bud Somerville, USA	1965, '74
Don Duguid, Canada	1970, '71
Rod Hunter, Canada	1970, '71
Jim Pettapiece, Canada	1970, '71
Bryan Wood, Canada	1970, '71
Bob Nichols, USA	1974, '78
Tom Locken, USA	1974, '78
Eigil Ramsfjell, Norway	1979, '84
Gunnar Meland, Norway	1979, '84
Al Hackner, Canada	1982, '85
Rick Lang, Canada	1982, '85

Highest Number of World Curling Appearances

Name	No.	Years
Andrea Pavani, Italy	11	1973, '74, '76, '77, '79, '80, '81, '82, '84, '85, '86
Pierre Boan, France	9	1967, '68, '69, '70, '71, '72, '73, '77, '78
Eigil Ramsfjell, Norway	8	1976, '77, '78, '79, '80, '81, '83, '84
Gunner Meland, Norway	8	1976, '77, '78, '79, '80, '81, '83, '84
Giuseppe Dal Molin, Italy	7	1975, '76, '77, '79, '80, '81, '83
Enea Pavani, Italy	7	1975, '76, '77, '79, '80, '81, '82
Giancarlo Valt, Italy	7	1977, '79, '80, '81, '82, '84, '85
Kristan Sorum, Norway	7	1976, '77, '78, '79, '80, '81, '85
Keith Wendorf, Germany	7	1978, '79, '81, '82, '83, '84, '85
André Trone, France	6	1971, '72, '73, '75, '76, '82

8 tied with 5

World Curling

	Appearances	Games Won
Eigil Ramsfjell, Norway	8	56
Gunner Meland, Norway	8	56
Kristian Soerum, Norway	7	45
Keith Wendorf, Germany	7	36
Bill Strum, USA	5	34
Andrea Pavani, Italy	11	33
Bud Sommerville, USA	5	32
Bruce Roberts, USA	5	31

6 tied with 25 wins— 3 members of Chuck Hay, Scotland; 3 members of Keith Wendorf, Germany

4 tied with 24 wins— R. Lang, Canada; B. Woods, Canada; B. Nichols, U.S.A.; G. Valt, Italy.

 What province leads in Brier Championships but did not win the Canadian Men's Junior Championship till 1979, some 29 years into that competition? Answer: Manitoba. This province has won 22 Briers, and finally, in 1979, the Mert Thompsett rink of Manitoba won the Juniors'.

Can a fast runner keep up to the very fastest curling rock? The bets were laid, as we went out on to the ice to test the theory. Larry Frandsen, the runner (quickest feet around), stood on the backboards, behind and to the side of the thrower, poised to sprint with the downswing of the rock. Fast Eddie was the thrower and he could really hum one because of his youthful days of natural-ice curling. The speeding rock and Larry were off. Who won the race to the far end, Larry or the rock?

Most folk would bet on the fast-thrown rock outracing a speedy runner down a sheet of curling ice. They would lose the bet. Although the rock has high velocity in the first half of the race, it loses pace as it nears the far hog line. The running man starts slowly until the first hog. However, the runner accelerates at the mid-point and after reaching top speed he is able to catch and overtake the failing stone before the rings.

Brier All-Stars
* indicates Brier winner

1965
Lead   R.Turnbull, Man.*
Second K. Hamilton, Alta.
Third   D. Duguid, Man.*
Skip   J. Polyblank, N. Ont.

1966
Lead   F. Storey, Alta.*
Second B. Sparkes, Alta.*
Third   T. Howat, Ont.
Skip   R. Northcott, Alta.*

1967
Lead   K. Reilly, Ont.*
Second B. Sparkes, Alta.
Third   G. Fink, Alta.
Skip   D. Wankel, Sask.

1968
Lead   F. Storey, Alta.*
Second B. Sparkes, Alta.*
Third   J. Keys, Sask.
Skip   R. Northcott, Alta.*

1969
Lead   F. Storey, Alta.*
Second B. Sparkes, Alta.*
Third   P. Sherba, B.C.
Skip   R. Northcott, Alta.*

1970
Lead   G. Ford, Sask.
Second L. Hebert, B.C.
Third   J. Carson, N. Ont.
Skip   D. Duguid, Man.*

1971
Lead   G. Ford, Sask.
Second J. Pettapiece, Man.*
Third   R. Hunter, Man.*
Skip   B. Tetley, N. Ont.

1972
Lead   M. Gregga, Que.
Second T. Watchhorn, Alta.
Third   D. Romano, Man.*
Skip   B. Kent, Que.

1973
Lead   R. Green, Ont.
Second D. Romkey, N.B.
Third   B. Martin, Sask.*
Skip   H. Mazinke, Sask.*

1974
Lead   R. Green, Ont.
Second G. Peckham, B.C.
Third   R. Anton, Alta.*
Skip   J. Ursel, Que.

1975
Lead   H. Atkinson, Que.
Second M. Boyd, Ont.
Third   B. Martin, Sask.
Skip   D. Twa, Terr

1976
Lead   K. Bauer, B.C.
Second D. Aitken, Que.
Third   B. Gretzinger, B.C.
Skip   J. MacDuff, Nfld.*

1977
Lead   B. Collez, Man.
Second L. Stokes, Terr.
Third   A. Lobel, Que.*
Skip   J. Ursel, Que.*

1978
Lead   K. Bauer, B.C.
Second A. Cook, B.C.
Third   M. Chernoff, Alta.*
Skip   R. Folk, Sask.

1979
Lead   B. Wood, Man.*
Second G. Campbell, N. Ont.
Third   B. Carey, Man.*
Skip   B. Fry, Man.*

1980
Lead   J. Wilson, Sask.*
Second T. Wilson, Sask.*
Third   N. Houston, Alta.
Skip   R. Folk, Sask.*

1981
Lead   J. McGrath, Ont.
Second R. Weigand, Que.
Third   M. Olson, Man.*
Skip   A. Hackner, N. Ont.

1982
Lead   W. Rechenmacher, Sask.
Second A. Roemer, B.C.
Third   D. Armour, Man.
Skip   A. Hackner, N. Ont.*

1983
Lead   N. Harrison, Ont.*
Second J. Kawaja, Ont.*
Third   P. Savage, Ont.*
Skip   E. Lukowich, Alta.

1984
Lead   N. Harrison, Ont.
Second W. Foss, Sask.
Third   D. Graham, Sask.
Skip   M. Riley, Man.*

1985
Lead   B. Fletcher, Ont.
Second D. McKenzie, Alta.
Third   D. Iverson, Man.
Skip   P. Ryan, Alta.

1986
Lead   G. Muyres, Sask.
Second C. Muyres, Sask.
Third   G. Howard, Ont.
Skip   E. Lukowich, Alta.*

Ladies' Curling Trivia

Who has had the most appearances in the Canadian Ladies' Championships?
Answer: Sue Anne Bartlett of Labrador, Newfoundland, with 10.

Most Canadian Ladies' Curling Championships
5 by Joyce McKee, Saskatoon, Saskatchewan, 1961, '69 (both as skip), '71, '72, '73 (at second).
4 by Vera Pezer, Saskatoon, Saskatchewan, 1969 (third), '71,'72, '73 (skip).
4 by Lenore Morrison, Saskatoon, Saskatchewan, 1969 (second), '71, '72, '73 (lead).
3 by Sheila Rowan, Saskatoon, Saskatchewan, 1971, '72, '73 (third).
3 by Lindsay Sparkes, 1976, '79 (skip), 1985 (third).
Only team to win 3 consecutive Canadian Ladies' Championships—Vera Pezer (skip), Sheila Rowan (third), Joyce McKee (second), Lenore Morrison (lead), 1971, '72, '73.

Senior Men's, Most Canadian Championships

3 times Canadian Senior Champion—consecutive 1982, '83, '84. Lloyd Gunnalangson (Manitoba) skip, Toru Suzuki (third), Albert Olson (second).

Senior Ladies', Most Canadian Championships

4 times—Flora Martin, B.C. (skip) and Edna Messum (third), 1974, '75, '79, '80.
3 times—consecutive 1984, '85, '86. Ev Krahn, Sask. (skip), Twyla Widdifield (third), Shirley Little (second), June Kaufman (lead).

Most World Junior Titles

2—Paul Gowsell, Calgary (skip),1976, '78.

Mixed Championships

3 times champions—Larry McGrath, Sask. (skip), John Gunn, Sask.(second), Darlene Hill, Sask.(third), 1967, '68, '71.

Canadian Junior Women's Champions

1971	Alberta	Shelby McKenzie, Marlene Pargeter, Arlene Hrdlicka, Debbie Goliss
1972	Manitoba	Chris Pidzarko, Cathy Pidzarko, Beth Brunsden, Barbara Rudolph
1973	Saskatchewan	Janet Crimp, Carol Davis, Chris Gervais, Susan Carney
1974	Manitoba	Chris Pidzarko, Cathy Pidzarko, Patti Vanderkerckhove, Barbara Rudolph
1975	Saskatchewan	Patricia Crimp, Colleen Rudd, Judy Sefton, Merrill Greabelel
1976	Saskatchewan	Colleen Rudd, Carol Rudd, Julie Burke, Lori Glenn
1977	Alberta	Cathy King, Robin Ursuliak, Maureen Olsen, Mary Kay James
1978	Alberta	Cathy King, Brenda Oko, Maureen Olsen, Diane Bowes
1979	Saskatchewan	Denise Wilson, Judy Walker, Dianne Choquette, Shannon Olafson
1980	Nova Scotia	Kay Smith, Krista Gatchell, Cathy Caudle, Peggy Wilson
1981	Manitoba	Karen Fallis, Karen Tresoor, Caroline Hunter, Lynn Fallis
1982	British Columbia	Sandra Plut, Sandra Rainey, Leigh Fraser, Debra Fowles
1983	Ontario	Alison Goring, Kristin Holman, Cheryl McPherson, Lynda Armstrong
1984	Manitoba	Darcy Kirkness, Barb Kirkness, Janet Harvey, Barbara Fetch
1985	Saskatchewan	Kimberley Armbruster, Sheila Calcutt, Wanda Figgitt, Lorraine Krupski
1986	British Columbia	Judie Sutton, Julie Sutton, Dawn Rubner, Chris Thompson

Canadian Senior Ladies' Champions

1973	British Columbia	Ada Calles, Ina Hansen, Mae Shaw, Barbara Weir
1974	British Columbia	Flora Martin, Edna Messum, Doreen Baker, Betty Stubbs
1975	British Columbia	Flora Martin, Edna Messum, Doreen Baker, Betty Stubbs
1976	Alberta	Hadie Manley, Bernie Durward, Anna Kasting, Gladys Baptist
1977	British Columbia	Vi Tapella, Rose Neratini, Doris Driesche, Mary Lee Bacchus
1978	Alberta	Hadie Manley, Bernie Durward, Dee McIntyre, Anna Kasting
1979	British Columbia	Flora Martin, Elsie Humphrey, Verle McKeown, Edna Messum
1980	British Columbia	Flora Martin, Elsie Humphrey, Verle McKeown, Edna Messum
1981	Alberta	Bea Mayer, Eileen Cyr, Leah Nate, Alice Vejprava
1982	Nova Scotia	Verda Kempton, Lucille Hamm, Molly Pirie, Lois Smith
1983	Manitoba	Mabel Mitchell, Mary Adams, Mildred Murray, June Clark
1984	Saskatchewan	Ev Krahn, Twyla Widdifield, Shirley Little, June Kaufman
1985	Saskatchewan	Ev Krahn, Twyla Widdifield, Shirley Little, June Kaufman
1986	Saskatchewan	Ev Krahn, Twyla Widdifield, Shirley Little, June Kaufman

Canadian Senior Men's Champions

Seagram Stone Champions

1965	Manitoba	Leo Johnson, Marno Frederickson, Fred Smith, Cliff Wise
1966	Ontario	Jim Johnston, Tom Rosborough, Joe Todd, Ed Waller
1967	New Brunswick	Jim Murphy, Harry Farrell, Don Beatteay, Walter Biddiscombe
1968	Saskatchewan	Don Wilson, Carson Tufts, Ivan McMillan, Reuben Lowe
1969	Ontario	Alfie Phillips, George Cowan, Sandy McTavish, Jack Young
1970	British Columbia	Don MacRae, Gene Koster, Bev Smiley, Doc Howden
1971	Prince Edward I.	Wen MacDonald, John Squarebriggs, Doug George, Dan O'Rourke
1972	Quebec	Ken Weldon, Ben McCormick, Bob Hubbard, Larry Elliott
1973	Manitoba	Bill McTavish, Bunt McLean, John McLean, Harry Sulkers
1974	British Columbia	George Beaudry, Buzz McGibney, Tom Clark, Harvey McKay

C.C.A. Senior Champions

1975	Prince Edward I.	Wen MacDonald, John Squarebriggs, Irvine MacKinnon, Don Hutchison
1976	Prince Edward I.	Wen MacDonald, John Squarebriggs, Irvine MacKinnon, Don Hutchison
1977	Saskatchewan	Morrie Thompson, Bert Harbottle, Archie Bartley, Mac McKee
1978	Saskatchewan	Art Knutson, Ernie Vaughan, Gay Knutson, Elmer Knutson
1979	Alberta	Cliff Forry, John Wolfe, Fred Kalicum, Ray Wellman
1980	Saskatchewan	Terry McGeary, Don Berglind, Hillis Thompson, Clare Ramsey
1981	Quebec	Jim Wilson, Garth Ruiter, George Brown, Bert Skitt
1982	Manitoba	Lloyd Gunnlaugson, Toru Suzuki, Albert Olson, Elgin Christianson
1983	Manitoba	Lloyd Gunnlaugson, Toru Suzuki, Albert Olson, Dennis Reid

1984	Manitoba	Lloyd Gunnlaugson, Toru Suzuki, Albert Olson, Elgin Christianson
1985	Saskatchewan	Frank Scherich, Joe Golumbia, Wally Yudepski, Al Wasslen
1986	Ontario	Earle Hushagen, Joe Gurowka, Art Lobel, Bert Barogan

Canadian Mixed Curling Championships
O'Keefe Mixed Champions

1964	Manitoba	Ernie Boushy, Ina Light, Garry DeBlonde, Bea McKenzie
1965	Alberta	Lee Green, Kay Berreth, Shirley Salt, Vi Salt
1966	Manitoba	Ernie Boushy, Ina Light, Garry DeBlonde, Betty Hird
1967	Saskatchewan	Larry McGrath, Darlene Hill, Peter Gunn, Marlene Dorsett
1968	Saskatchewan	Larry McGrath, Darlene Hill, Peter Gunn, Marlene Dorsett
1969	Alberta	Don Anderson, Bernie Hunter, Bill Tainsh, Marion Weir
1970	Alberta	Bill Mitchell, Hadie Manley, Bill Tainsh, Connie Reeve
1971	Saskatchewan	Larry McGrath, Darlene Hill, John Gunn, Audrey St. John
1972	British Columbia	Trev Fisher, Gail Wren, Bryan Bettesworth, Louise Fisher

Seagram Mixed Champions

1973	Manitoba	Barry Fry, Peggy Casselman, Stephen Decter, Susan Lynch
1974	Saskatchewan	Rick Folk, Cheryl Stirton, Tom Wilson, Bonnie Orchard
1975	Alberta	Les Rowland, Audrey Rowland, Dan Schmaltz, Betty Schmaltz
1976	British Columbia	Tony Eberts, Elizabeth Short, Clark Glanville, Eleanor Short
1977	Manitoba	Harold Tanasichuk, Rose Tanasichuk, Jim Kirkness, Debbie Orr
1978	Saskatchewan	Bernie Yuzdepski, Marnie McNiven, Roy Uchman, Joan Bjerke, Ron Apland, Marsha Kerr
1979	Northern Ontario	Roy Lund, Nancy Lund, Ron Apland, Marsha Kerr
1980	Manitoba	Jim Dunstone, Carol Dunstone, Del Stitt, Elaine Jones
1981	Northern Ontario	Rick Lang, Anne Provo, Bert Provo, Lorraine Edwards
1982	British Columbia	Glen Pierce, Marlene Neubauer, Fuji Miki, Sharon Bradley
1983	Saskatchewan	Rick Folk, Dorenda Schoenhals, Tom Wilson, Elizabeth Folk
1984	Saskatchewan	Randy Woytowich, Kathy Fahlman, Brian McCusker, Jan Betker
1985	British Columbia	Steve Skillins, Pat Saunders, Allan Carlsen, Louise Herlinveaux
1986	Ontario	Dave Van Dive, Dawn Ventura, Hugh Millikin, Cindy Wiggins

Canadian Junior Men's Curling Championship
Victor Sifton Trophy Champions

1950	Saskatchewan	Bill Clarke, Gerry Carlson, Ian Innes, Harold Grassier
1951	Saskatchewan	Gary Thode, Gary Cooper, Orest Hymiuk, Roy Hufsmith
1952	Saskatchewan	Gary Thode, Gary Cooper, Doug Conn, Roy Hufsmith
1953	Ontario	Bob Walker, Duncan Brodie, Claire Peacock, George MacGregor
1954	Saskatchewan	Bayne Secord, Don Snider, Stan Austman, Don Brownell

1955	Saskatchewan	Bayne Secord, Stan Austman, Merv Mann, Gary Stevenson
1956	Saskatchewan	Bob Hawkins, Ted Clarke, Bruce Beveridge, Dave Williams
1957	Ontario	Ian Johnson, Peter Galsworthy, Dave Robinson, Mike Jackson

Pepsi-Cola Trophy Champions

1958	Prince Edward I.	Tom Tod, Neil McLeod, Patrick Moran, David Allin
1959	Alberta	John Trout, Bruce Walker, David Woods, Allen Sharpe
1960	Alberta	Tommy Kroeger, Jack Isaman, Ron Nelson, Murray Sorenson
1961	British Columbia	Jerry Caughlin, Jack Cox, Mike Shippitt, David Jones
1962	Saskatchewan	Mike Lukowich, Ed Lukowich, Doug McLeod, David Moore
1963	Alberta	Wayne Saboe, Ron Hampton, Rick Alridge, Mick Adams
1964	Ontario	Bob Ash, Bill Ash, Gerry Armstrong, Fred Prier
1965	Saskatchewan	Dan Fink, Ken Runtz, Ron Jacques, Larry Lechner
1966	Alberta	Brian Howes, Blair Pallesen, John Thompson, Chris Robinson
1967	Alberta	Stanley Trout, Doug Dobry, Allan Kullay, Donald Douglas
1968	Ontario	William Hope, Bruce Lord, Brian Domney, Dennis Gardiner
1969	Saskatchewan	Robert Miller, Roger Rask, Lloyd Helm, William Aug
1970	New Brunswick	Ronald Ferguson, Garth Jardine, Brian Henderson, Cyril Sutherland
1971	Saskatchewan	Greg Montgomery, Don Despins, Jeff Montgomery, Rod Verboom
1972	Alberta	Lawrence Niven, Rick Niven, Jim Ross, Ted Polblawski
1973	Ontario	Mark McDonald, Lloyd Emmerson, Phillip Tomsett, Jon Clare
1974	Alberta	Robb King, Brad Hannah, Bill Fowlis, Chris King
1975	Alberta	Paul Gowsell, Neil Houston, Glen Jackson, Kelly Stearne
1976	Prince Edward I.	Bill Jenkins, John Scales, Sandy Stewart, Alan Mayhew
1977	Alberta	Paul Gowsell, John Ferguson, Doug McFarlane, Kelly Stearne
1978	Alberta	Darren Fish, Lorne Barker, Murray Ursulak, Barry Barker
1979	Manitoba	Mert Thompsett, Lyle Derry, Joel Gagne, Mike Friesen
1980	Quebec	Denis Marchand, Denis Cecil, Yves Barrette, Larry Phillips
1981	Manitoba	Mert Thompsett, Bill McTavish, Joel Gagne, Mike Friesen
1982	Ontario	John Base, Bruce Webster, Dave McAnerney, Jim Donahoe
1983	Saskatchewan	Jamie Schneider, Danny Ferner, Steven Leippi, Kelly Vollman
1984	Manitoba	Bob Ursel, Brent Mandella, Gerald Chick, Mike Ursel
1985	Alberta	Kevin Martin, Rich Feeney, Daniel Petryk, Michael Berger
1986	Manitoba	Hugh McFadyen, Jonathan Mead, Norman Gould, John Lange

World Junior Champions (Men's)

1975	Sweden	Jan Ullsten, Mats Nyberg, Anders Grahn, Bo Soderstrom
1976	Canada	Paul Gowsell, Neil Houston, Glen Jackson, Kelly Stearne
1977	Canada	Bill Jenkins, John Scales, Sandy Stewart, Alan Mayhew
1978	Canada	Paul Gowsell, John Ferguson, Doug McFarlane, Kelly Stearne
1979	U.S.A.	Don Barcome, Randy Darling, Bobby Stalker, Earl Barcome
1980	Scotland	Andrew McQuistin, Norman Brown, Hugh Aitken, Dick Adams
1981	Scotland	Peter Wilson, Jim Cannon, Roger McIntyre, John Parker
1982	Sweden	Soren Grahn, Niklas Jarund, Henrik Holmberg, Anders Svennerstedt
1983	Canada	John Base, Bruce Webster, Dave McAnerney, Jim Donahoe
1984	U.S.A.	Al Edwards, Mark Larson, Dewey Basley, Kurt Disher
1985	Canada	Bob Ursel, Gerald Chick, Brent Mendella, Mike Ursel
1986	Scotland	David Aitken, Robin Halliday, Peter Smith, Harry Reilly

Canadian Ladies' Curling Champions

1961	Saskatchewan	Joyce McKee, Sylvia Fedoruk, Barbara MacNevin, Rose McFee
1962	British Columbia	Ina Hansen, Ada Callas, Isabel Leith, May Shaw
1963	New Brunswick	Mabel DeWare, Harriet Strattan, Forbis Stevenson, Majorie Fraser
1964	British Columbia	Ina Hansen, Ada Callas, Isabel Leith, May Shaw
1965	Manitoba	Peggy Casselman, Val Taylor, Pat MacDonald, Pat Scott
1966	Alberta	Gale Lee, Hazel Jamieson, Sharon Harrington, June Coyle
1967	Manitoba	Betty Duguid, Joan Ingram, Laurie Bradawaski, Dot Rose
1968	Alberta	Hazel Jamieson, Gale Lee, Jackie Spencer, June Coyle
1969	Saskatchewan	Joyce McKee, Vera Pezer, Lenore Morrison, Jennifer Falk
1970	Saskatchewan	Dorenda Schoenhals, Cheryl Stirton, Linda Burnham, Joan Anderson
1971	Saskatchewan	Vera Pezer, Sheila Rowan, Joyce McKee, Lenore Morrison
1972	Saskatchewan	Vera Pezer, Sheila Rowan, Joyce McKee, Lenore Morrison
1973	Saskatchewan	Vera Pezer, Sheila Rowan, Joyce McKee, Lenore Morrison
1974	Saskatchewan	Emily Farnham, Linda Saunders, Pat McBeth, Donna Collins
1975	Quebec	Lee Tobin, Marilyn McNeil, Michelle Garneau, Laurie Ross
1976	British Columbia	Lindsay Davis, Dawn Knowles, Robin Klasen, Lorraine Bowles
1977	Alberta	Myrna McQuarrie, Rita Tarnava, Barb Davis, Jane Rempel
1978	Manitoba	Cathy Pidzarko, Chris Pidzarko, Iris Armstrong, Patty Vande
1979	British Columbia	Lindsay Sparkes, Dawn Knowles, Robin Wilson, Lorraine Bowles
1980	Saskatchewan	Marj Mitchell, Nancy Kerr, Shirley McKendry, Wendy Leach
1981	Alberta	Susan Seitz, Judy Erickson, Myna McKay, Betty McCracken

Scott Tournament of Hearts Champions

1982	Nova Scotia	Colleen Jones, Kay Smith, Monica Jones, Barbara Jones-Gordon
1983	Nova Scotia	Penny LaRocque, Sharon Horne, Cathy Caudie, Pam Sanford
1984	Manitoba	Connie Laliberte, Chris More, Corinne Peters, Janet Arnott
1985	British Columbia	Linda Moore, Lindsay Sparkes, Debbie Jones, Laurie Carney
1986	Ontario	Marilyn Darte, Kathy McEdwards, Chris Jurgensen, Jan Augustyn

Ladies' World Champions

1979	Switzerland	Gaby Casanova, Rosie Manger, Linda Thommen, Betty Bourguin
1980	Canada	Marj Mitchell, Nancy Kerr, Shirley McKendry, Wendy Leach
1981	Sweden	Elisabeth Hogstrom, Carina Olsson, Birgitta Sewick, Karin Sjogren
1982	Denmark	Marianne Jorgensen, Helena Blach, Astrid Birnbaum, Jette Olsen
1983	Switzerland	Erika Mueller, Barbara Meyer, Barbara Meler, Christina Wirz
1984	Canada	Connie Laliberte, Chris More, Corinne Peters, Janet Arnott
1985	Canada	Linda Moore, Lindsay Sparkes, Debbie Jones, Laurie Carney
1986	Canada	Marilyn Darte, Kathy McEdwards, Chris Jurgenson, Jan Augustyn

Brier Champions

MacDonald Brier Champions

1928	Manitoba	Gordon Hudson, Sam Penwarden, Ron Singbusch, Bill Grant
1929	Manitoba	Gordon Hudson, Don Rollo, Ron Singbusch, Bill Grant
1930	Manitoba	Howard Wood, Jimmy Congalton, Victor Wood, Lionel Wood
1931	Manitoba	Bob Gourlay, Ernie Pollard, Arnold Lockerbie, Ray Stewart
1932	Manitoba	Jimmy Congalton, Howard Wood, Bill Noble, Harry Mawhinney
1933	Alberta	Cliff Manahan, Harold Deeton, Harold Wolfe, Bert Ross
1934	Manitoba	Leo Johnson, Lorne Stewart, Linc Johnson, Marno Frederickson
1935	Ontario	Gordon Campbell, Don Campbell, Gord Coates, Duncan Campbell
1936	Manitoba	Ken Watson, Grant Watson, Marvin McIntyre, Charles Kerr
1937	Alberta	Cliff Manahan, Wes Robinson, Ross Manahan, Lloyd McIntyre
1938	Manitoba	Ab Gowanlock, Bung Cartmell, Bill McKnight, Tom Knight
1939	Ontario	Bert Hall, Perry Hall, Ernie Parkes, Cam Seagram
1940	Manitoba	Howard Wood, Ernie Pollard, Howard Wood Jr., Roy Enman
1941	Alberta	Howard Palmer, Jack Lebeau, Art Gooder, Clare Webb
1942	Manitoba	Ken Watson, Grant Watson, Charlie Scrymgeour, Jim Grant
1946	Alberta	Billy Rose, Bart Swelin, Austin Smith, George Crooks
1947	Manitoba	Jimmy Welsh, Alex Walsh, Jack Reid, Harry Monk
1948	British Columbia	Frenchy D'Amour, Bob McGhle, Fred Wendell, Jim Mark
1949	Manitoba	Ken Watson, Grant Watson, Lyle Dyker, Charles Read
1950	Northern Ontario	Tom Ramsay, Len Williamson, Bill Weston, Bill Kenny

1951	Nova Scotia	Don Oyler, George Hanson, Fred Dyke, Wally Knock
1952	Manitoba	Billy Walsh, Al Langlois, Andy McWilliams, John Watson
1953	Manitoba	Al Gowanlock, Jim Williams, Art Pollon, Russ Jackman
1954	Alberta	Matt Baldwin, Glen Gray, Pete Ferry, Jim Collins
1955	Saskatchewan	Garnet Campbell, Don Campbell, Glen Campbell, Lloyd Campbell
1956	Manitoba	Billy Walsh, Al Langlois, Cy White, Andy McWilliams
1957	Alberta	Matt Baldwin, Gordon Haynes, Art Kleinmeyer, Bill Price
1958	Alberta	Matt Baldwin, Jack Geddes, Gordon Haynes, Bill Price
1959	Saskatchewan	Ernie Richardson, Arnold Richardson, Sam Richardson, Wes Richardson
1960	Saskatchewan	Ernie Richardson, Arnold Richardson, Sam Richardson, Wes Richardson
1961	Alberta	Hec Gervais, Ron Anton, Ray Werner, Wally Ursullak
1962	Saskatchewan	Ernie Richardson, Arnold Richardson, Sam Richardson, Wes Richardson
1963	Saskatchewan	Ernie Richardson, Arnold Richardson, Sam Richardson, Mel Perry
1964	British Columbia	Lyall Dagg, Leo Hebert, Fred Britton, Barry Naimark
1965	Manitoba	Terry Braunstein, Don Duguid, Ron Braunstein, Ray Turnbull
1966	Alberta	Ron Northcott, George Fink, Bernie Sparkes, Fred Storey
1967	Ontario	Alf Phillips Jr., John Ross, Ron Manning, Keith Reilly
1968	Alberta	Ron Northcott, Jim Shields, Bernie Sparkes, Fred Storey
1969	Alberta	Ron Northcott, Dave Gerlach, Bernie Sparkes, Fred Storey
1970	Manitoba	Don Duguid, Rod Hunter, Jim Pettapiece, Bryan Wood
1971	Manitoba	Don Duguid, Rod Hunter, Jim Pettapiece, Bryan Wood
1972	Manitoba	Orest Meleschuk, Dave Romano, John Hanesiak, Pat Hailley
1973	Saskatchewan	Harvey Mazinke, Bill Martin, George Achtymichuk, Dan Klippenstein
1974	Alberta	Hec Gervais, Ron Anton, Warren Hansen, Darrel Sutton
1975	Northern Ontario	Bill Tetley, Rick Lang, Bill Hodgson, Peter Hnatiew
1976	Newfoundland	Jack MacDuff, Toby McDonald, Doug Hudson, Ken Templeton
1977	Quebec	Jim Ursel, Art Lobel, Don Aitken, Brian Ross
1978	Alberta	Ed Lukowich, Mike Chernoff, Dale Johnson, Ron Schindle
1979	Manitoba	Barry Fry, Bill Carey, Gord Sparkes, Bryan Wood

Labatt Brier Champions

1980	Saskatchewan	Rick Folk, Ron Mills, Tom Wilson, Jim Wilson
1981	Manitoba	Kerry Burtnyk, Mark Olson, Jim Spencer, Ron Kammerlock
1982	Northern Ontario	Al Hackner, Rick Lang, Bob Nicol, Bruce Kennedy
1983	Ontario	Ed Werenich, Paul Savage, John Kawaja, Neil Harrison
1984	Manitoba	Mike Riley, Brian Toews, John Halston, Russ Wookey
1985	Northern Ontario	Al Hackner, Rick Lang, Ian Tetley, Pat Perroud
1986	Alberta	Ed Lukowich, John Ferguson, Neil Houston, Brent Syme

Brier Attendance

1946	Saskatoon	22,000
1947	Saint John	10,000
1948	Calgary	30,000
1949	Hamilton	16,500
1950	Vancouver	25,000
1951	Halifax	17,000
1952	Winnipeg	12,500
1953	Sudbury	22,000
1954	Edmonton	32,000
1955	Regina	51,725
1956	Moncton	25,800
1957	Kingston	19,000
1958	Victoria	36,000
1959	Quebec City	16,000
1960	Fort William	26,000
1961	Calgary	51,575
1962	Kitchener	37,013
1963	Brandon	42,113
1964	Charlottetown	13,573
1965	Saskatoon	52,319
1966	Halifax	11,905
1967	Ottawa	26,174
1968	Kelowna	25,813
1969	Oshawa	28,446
1970	Winnipeg	60,255
1971	Quebec City	8,501
1972	St. John's	12,890
1973	Edmonton	37,575
1974	London	48,170
1975	Fredericton	20,672
1976	Regina	61,110
1977	Montreal	50,000*
1978	Vancouver	63,851
1979	Ottawa	89,081
1980	Calgary	93,185
1981	Halifax	67,257
1982	Brandon	106,394+
1983	Sudbury	65,927
1984	Victoria	86,811
1985	Moncton	65,475
1986	Kitchener	102,303

*estimate
+record

Men's World Curling Champions

Scotch Cup Champions

1959	Canada	Ernie Richardson, Arnold Richardson, Sam Richardson, Wes Richardson
1960	Canada	Ernie Richardson, Arnold Richardson, Sam Richardson, Wes Richardson
1961	Canada	Hector Gervais, Ray Werner, Vic Raymer, Wally Ursullak
1962	Canada	Ernie Richardson, Arnold Richardson, Sam Richardson, Wes Richardson
1963	Canada	Ernie Richardson, Arnold Richardson, Sam Richardson, Mel Perry
1964	Canada	Lyall Dagg, Leo Hebert, Fred Britton, Barry Nalmark
1965	U.S.A.	Bud Somerville, Bill Strum, Al Gagne, Tom Wright
1966	Canada	Ron Northcott, George Fink, Bernie Sparkes, Fred Storey
1967	Scotland	Chuck Hay, John Bryden, Alan Glen, David Howie

Air Canada Silver Broom Champions

1968	Canada	Ron Northcott, Jimmy Shields, Bernie Sparkes, Fred Storey
1969	Canada	Ron Northcott, Dave Gerlach, Bernie Sparkes, Fred Storey
1970	Canada	Don Duguid, Rod Hunter, Jim Pettapiece, Bryan Wood
1971	Canada	Don Duguid, Rod Hunter, Jim Pettapiece, Bryan Wood
1972	Canada	Orest Meleschuk, Dave Romano, John Haneslak, Pat Hailley
1973	Sweden	Kjell Oscarlus, Bengt Oscarlus, Tom Schaeffer, Boa Carlman
1974	U.S.A.	Bud Somerville, Bob Nichols, Bill Strum, Tom Locken
1975	Switzerland	Otto Daniell, Roland Schneider, Rolf Gautschi, Uell Mulli
1976	U.S.A.	Bruce Roberts, Joe Roberts, Gary Kleffman, Jerry Scott
1977	Sweden	Ragner Kamp, Hakan Rudstrom, Bjorn Rudstrom, Christer Martensson
1978	U.S.A.	Bob Nichols, Bill Strum, Tom Locken, Bob Christman
1979	Norway	Kristian Soerum, Morten Soerum, Eigil Ramsfjell, Gunnar Meland
1980	Canada	Rick Folk, Ron Mills, Tom Wilson, Jim Wilson
1981	Switzerland	Jurg Tanner, Jurg Hornisberger, Patrick Loerfscher, Franz Tanner
1982	Canada	Al Hackner, Rick Lang, Bob Nichol, Bruce Kennedy
1983	Canada	Ed Werenich, Paul Savage, John Kawaja, Neil Harrison
1984	Norway	Eigil Ramsfjell, Sjur Loen, Gunnar Meland, Bo Bakke
1985	Canada	Allan Hackner, Rick Lang, Ian Tetley, Pat Perroud

President's Cup

1986	Canada	Ed Lukowich, John Ferguson, Neil Houston, Brent Syme

World Championships Won (Country)

	World Men's	World Ladies'	World Junior Men's	Total
Canada	17	4	5	26
Switzerland	2	2		4
Sweden	2	1	2	5
Denmark		1		1
Norway	2			2
France				
Italy				
Scotland	1		3	4
Finland				
U.S.A.	4		2	6
England				
Netherlands				
Number of years held	28	8	12	48

M.B.

Paul Gowsell of Calgary, Alberta, the only two-time Uniroyal Junior Champion.

Canadian Championship Totals

	Men's Brier	Ladies' Scotts	Senior Men's	Senior Ladies'	Junior Men's	Junior Women's	Mixed	Total
British Columbia	2	5	2	6	1	2	4	22
Alberta	14	4	1	3	11	3	4	40
The Territories	0	0	0	0	0	0	0	0
Saskatchewan	7	8	5	3	11	5	7	46
Manitoba	22	4	5	1	4	4	5	45
Northern Ontario	4	0	0	0	0	0	2	6
Ontario	4	1	3	0	6	1	1	16
Quebec	1	1	2	1	1	0	0	6
Nova Scotia	2	2	0	0	0	1	0	5
New Brunswick	0	1	1	0	1	0	0	3
Prince Edward I.	0	0	3	0	2	0	0	5
Newfoundland	1	0	0	0	0	0	0	1
YEARS HELD	57	26	22	14	37	16	23	195

Saskatchewan with its 1986 victory in the senior ladies (Evelyn Krahn with her third straight title) moved Saskatchewan ahead of Manitoba as the top province for Canadian championship curling. The Territories remain 46 titles behind. They are the only region that has not won a Canadian curling title.

M.B.

Olympians in the making? The Olympic camps could provide tough competition. Any curler in Canada can make it to the Olympics by finishing high in the Ladies' or Men's Canadian Championships and winning at the Olympic trials.

A Short History of Curling

There are close to two million curlers in Canada, compared to nearly 50,000 in Scotland, the traditional homeland of this sport. Both Holland and Scotland claim to be the homelands of curling. It was first depicted as a sport by the Flemish painter Pieter Bruegel (1525-1569). However, the development of the sport is definitely to be credited to the Scots. The first Scottish club was formed in 1510.

The history of curling is rich in drama, comedy, thrills, tiffs, regal frowns, and royal edicts. King James, back in 1565, was in the doghouse with Queen Mary for withholding the crown matrimonial, and so Jimmy, in a sullen mood, went to a place called Peebles with a few congenial associates. A heavy snowfall detained him there and according to legend, he relieved the tedium of the time by curling on a flooded meadow. In fact a curling stone with the date 1551 inscribed on it was found many years ago, when an old curling pond was drained near Dunblane, Perthshire, Scotland.

The Canadian side of the story doesn't unfold until nearly two centuries later. Back in 1760 the 78th Highlanders under General Murray played the game on the St. Charles River while they were convalescing from their battle at Ste. Foy, Quebec. They melted down cannonballs to mould the stone-shaped objects. They were called irons and the oldest curling club in Canada, the Royal Montreal, which started in 1807, had many members who preferred the "iron" game to stone. Other areas saw it played with circular wooden objects with metal striking bands.

The Rideau Curling Club was established in a meeting held on November 10, 1888, in the Haycock Office, Sparks Street, Ottawa. There were competitions for the Governor General's Cup and awards. The first home of the RCC was a round-roofed quonset-hut type of building on the present campus of the University of Ottawa.

In 1838 Scotland's Grand Caledonian Curling Club was established, later to be renamed the Royal Caledonian Curling Club after an exhibition game for the young Queen Victoria.

At the 1932 Olympics in Lake Placid, New York, the Canadian team from Manitoba, led by J. Bowman, won the exhibition match. The world championship, held since 1959, was won by Canada six times in a row before the U.S.A. (1965) and Scotland (1967) had a chance at the title.

The game has been compared to shuffleboard or bowls. The major differences between these games and curling are that the latter is played on ice, and the player is able to influence the speed and course of the curling stone after it has left his hand. This technique was called "sooping," and consists of sweeping the ice in the path of the rock.

In Canada from time to time during the last century efforts were made to establish a curling association that would be representative at the national level of all provincial and other regional curling organizations. But it was not until 1935 that the Dominion Curling Association was founded. In 1968 it became the Canadian Curling Association. Then in 1972 the CCA was made a corporation.

The Brier was first held in 1927 and has been contested every year except for the war years 1943, 1944 and 1945. Since then, championships have been held in ladies', mixed, juniors' and seniors', and many job-related championships are also held, such as police, firefighters', etc.

The I.C.F. (International Curling Federation) had its beginning in 1968 and is the central body for the world curling championship.

Curl Canada began in 1974 as an association that would offer direction to curling in Canada. It has been a leader in developing international programs and helping the growth of the sport. This growth is becoming increasingly obvious. The Canadian Olympics held in Calgary in 1988 will have curling as a demonstrator sport. It is hoped that curling will be a full Olympic sport by 1992.

M.B.

So, keep sweeping hard, and remember to
begin and end every game with a friendly
handshake.

M.B.

...and happy trails.